This book is dedicated to my Mother and Father who had the wisdom and persever
reluctant sons to Europe by sea, not once but twice.
A second and equally important dedication is to Jennifer and Laurence Dunn, who
1964 and who opened my eyes to appreciating ships in so many new ways during m
both Kew and Gravesend.

Ocean Liner Odyssey 1958-1969

by

Theodore W. Scull

Published by

Carmania Press

Unit 202, Station House, 49 Greenwich High Road, London SE10 8JL, Great Britain.

ISBN 0 9518656 9 2 First published 1998
British Library Cataloguing for Publication Data.
A Catalogue Record for this book is available from the British Library.

Artwork production by Alan Kittridge.
Printed by The Amadeus Press Ltd., Huddersfield, Yorkshire.

Contents

Acknowledgements

I wish to thank my wife Suellyn who has patiently endured so much ship talk and who has seen me disappear day after day behind the computer on ship business; my brother Sandy for accompanying me on the *Liberté*, *Flandre*, *Bremen* and *Sampiero Corso* and for succumbing to mal de mer only 50 per cent of the time; Anthony Cooke, my publisher, who once asked, "Why haven't you written a book on ocean liners?"; Vincent Messina who shared with me not only his extensive knowledge but lent many brochures, deck plans and photographs; again, Laurence Dunn for his incomparable repository of photographs; Lady Jane (Macrae) for suggesting the French Line in the first place and then seeing to it that we were well treated on both crossings; Arthur Ferguson whom I met on board the P&O *Oriana* and who so generously shared his photographs from the 1940s and 1950s; and Charles N. Dragonette, Alan Kittridge and Alan Zamchick for many of the other illustrations in this book.

Apart from my journals which provided most of the material, for hard ship information I used both editions of Laurence Dunn's Passenger Liners; Arnold Kludas' seven volume series of Great Passenger Ships of the World; the ABC Shipping Guide, and of course, company literature provided by Adriatica, Cunard, French Line, Hamburg-Atlantic, Holland America, Italian Line, Navigation Mixte, North German Lloyd, Northland Navigation, Royal Mail, Swedish American Line, Swedish Lloyd.

FRONT COVER: **The *France* arriving at Southampton on the 31st August, 1973.** *Theodore W. Scull.*
BACK COVER: **The menu for the Farewell Dinner on the *Rotterdam*, 21st September, 1966.** *Author's Collection.*
FRONTICE: **The great flared bow of the *Flandre*, one of the author's favourite ships, here seen at Le Havre.** *Laurence Dunn Collection.*

Introduction

My very first memory of seeing a ship is of one evening at the tail end of World War II. For two consecutive summers, my brother Sandy, our nurse Bee and I spent a fortnight at Avalon on the New Jersey coast. Returning along the boardwalk following a film, I asked Bee about the flashing lights out at sea, and she said that they came from US warships signalling to each other. During the day I could see them better, and at times there were thunderous booms from firing guns but I never actually saw any of this.

Beginning in 1947, we began spending the month of August through Labour Day on Nantucket Island. On the long drive to and from Philadelphia I got to see close up the big liners docked in New York.

In those days, we entered New York via the Pulaski Skyway, an aerial roadway spanning the New Jersey Meadowlands that led down through the Holland Tunnel. As we reached the halfway point beneath the Hudson River, I remember my Father saying something like, "I wonder if the *Queen Mary* is sailing today, because if it's low tide, the propellers just might come chopping right through the ceiling." It left its mark and I think about this terrifying possibility when passing through, even today.

Arriving in Manhattan, we drove up the Canal Street ramp to the elevated West Side Highway, and from there you could see the entire skyline laid out to the right and the long string of finger piers jutting out into the river to the left. The Chelsea Piers were occupied mostly by cargo liners, some 'combi' ships belonging to the Grace Line, Panama Line and Moore-McCormack, and railway-owned car floats bringing freight wagons over from waterfront terminals in New Jersey. The big show would begin in the West Forties. From the south, the scene ahead was a dense forest of funnels, upright and angled, many banded and some bearing crowns.

Pop knew most of the lines from weekly trips to New York in connection with the coffee and tea business, and long before that when he sailed with his family to Europe.

The ships' bows practically hung over the elevated highway, and it was easy to read their names, while the pier head houses read: American Export Lines, United States Lines to all Europe; North German Lloyd, Greek Line, French Line, Italian Line, Cunard Line at two piers, and finally Home Lines, Furness Bermuda and Swedish American Line at the top end. Opposite Pier 95, Pop would say, "That's where your Mother and I sailed on the *Queen of Bermuda* on our honeymoon in 1936."

The activity at the piers was intense on 31st July, especially around noon when we passed by. As the roadway climbed a bit higher past the New York Central car float piers, I looked through the back window to watch the stacks recede. We didn't see salt water again until we reached New Bedford, Massachusetts, and by that time it was dark. From our hotel window, I could look down on the Nantucket steamer, either the *Martha's Vineyard* or *Nantucket*, a pair built in the mid-1920s at Bath Iron Works, a famous yard well up the New England

The New England Steamship Company's 1924-built *Martha's Vineyard*, seen here on 27th July, 1941, carried cargo, mail, vehicles, and passengers between New Bedford, Wood's Hole and the islands of Martha's Vineyard and Nantucket for over three decades. *Steamship Historical Society of America.*

coast in Maine. The steamboat stayed overnight, to leave early the next morning for the four and one-half hour run to Oaks Bluff on the Vineyard and on to Nantucket.

Pop invariably made the steamer reservations on 2nd January, the day the books opened for the summer season, because 1st August was a big turnover day for house rentals and so was the second day after Labour Day when we left the island.

We were nearly always among the first in line to drive on, which also often meant being about the last to get off upon reaching the island. Once aboard, my job was to take the cocker spaniel up to the purser's office and get the stateroom key. The day cabins were plainly furnished with a couch, a couple of folding canvas chairs, a washbasin and mirror and a button to call the stewardess for ice. The stateroom was a refuge on the crowded boat and it gave Father and Mother, who had driven a separate car with my younger brother and the cook, some peace between the 12-hour drive and opening a house for the summer.

The *Andrea Doria*, which sank off Nantucket in July, 1956 after a collision with the Swedish American Line's *Stockholm*. The 29,000-ton Italian luxury liner, which had a career of not much more than three years, is here seen at her home port of Genoa. Behind her are the funnels of one of her American Export Lines rivals, either the *Independence* or the *Constitution*. *Laurence Dunn Collection.*

I didn't stay inside for long because I liked to watch the departure. A few years later when the boats switched to a Wood's Hole terminal on the Cape, I enjoyed seeing the New Haven Railroad's *Cape Codder* come through the cut and stop at the end of the pier. People poured off the train with luggage and children in tow and made straight for the gangway.

From my position aft, I could see the whistle's steam billow upward to announce our departure. Under foot, I felt the prop turning and as we eased away from the pier, a wash piled up against the sea wall. Rounding Nobska Light, the boat entered Nantucket Sound and summer had officially begun.

About three-quarters of an hour later, we turned into Oaks Bluff, a village first built as a tented Methodist summer camp, then rebuilt into a gingerbread Victorian resort with a large green facing the steamboat wharf. During the 45-minute layover, boys about my age swam alongside to beg for coins, and we delighted in watching mid-air catches, or if missed, see them dive and usually resurface proudly holding a silver coin. Without fail, they would say 'thank you' before storing it in their bulging cheeks.

Underway again, we headed out past Chappaquiddick Island, and my favourite moment came, if the day was ever so slightly hazy, when for a brief couple of minutes, there was no land in sight. At the Cross Rip Lightship, the crew tossed over the mail and magazines, and the next serious activity involved picking out the black cylindrical Wanacomet water tower, the tallest structure on Nantucket. A few minutes later, we could see our house high on the cliff, standing out because of its reddish roof. The first sound of arrival was the clanging bell buoy at the entrance to the stone jetties leading to the harbour. Rounding Brandt Point Lighthouse the steamer whistled its arrival and dead ahead the town rose behind a large wooden shingled steamboat wharf.

It took a long time to dock, because the boat first had to go alongside the end of the wharf, then, using spring lines, swing around the corner pilings to have the bow point outward for departure. It was all bustle and activity getting back down to the car deck and then waiting to be one of the last to drive off. Sometimes, I got to disembark via the passenger gangway so the dog, by now bursting with excitement, could head for a convenient bollard.

Once settled in our cliffside house, I loved the routine of watching the steamers appear over the horizon in the early afternoon about 90 minutes apart. In the evening, one would arrive all lit up, then at 7 a.m. the next morning, the whistle signalled its departure. On foggy days, the morning steamer would blow its way out of the harbour, sounding every minute for about a quarter of an hour until the whistle grew too faint to hear.

Meeting someone arriving on the island was always a big event, and when friends left, we saw them off at the wharf then raced around on our bikes to Brandt Point to wave once more. Leaving for the summer, most people, usually the tourists, threw a coin overboard at Brandt Point, while others waited for the bell buoy, the last tangible link to the island.

In 1955, my parents left my brother and me for about six weeks, sailing to Europe on the *Queen Mary* and coming home on the *Andrea Doria*. Then the following summer while we were on Nantucket, the liner *Stockholm* and the *Andrea Doria* collided and the latter sank. Several days later bits and pieces came through the surf at the South Shore.

Some of our friends were aboard, but while they came away unscathed, their Volkswagen Beetle went to the bottom. They finally arrived on the island, but it wasn't until I went back to boarding school that autumn that I heard the full story from two of the three sons who also attended St. George's.

The school, set on a hill overlooking the sea, put me in touch with a maritime climate for the better part of three years. It was here that I took a fancy to fog, hurricanes and nor'easters, usually winter storms that came from that direction rather than from the south.

The best part of the trip to and from school was the Jamestown to Newport ferry. The boats were built in the same year I was born as I am reminded occasionally, because the ferryboat *Jamestown* resides just across the Hudson from Manhattan, serving as a terminal for the Weehawken to West 38th Street New York Waterway ferry.

I remember seeing my grandmother off on the *Independence* in 1958, an easy date to remember because I have the round red leather jewel box that she was given as a souvenir sitting on my desk. The gold lettering reads "Springtime Cruise *S.S. Independence* 1958." 39 springs later, I sailed aboard this ship in the Hawaiian islands.

1958 was also the year that Mother took her two sons to Europe. When the idea was first broached, I was not too keen because I had a paying job awaiting me at the Nantucket Cottage Hospital. But then in December, I underwent a spinal fusion, and the surgeon said that I would not be able to do the ambulance work or to lift patients.

So the die was cast, and Mother took out a loan to take her two boys to Europe, in style, via the French Line - First Class. That summer was a great adventure, and it opened the whole new world of sea travel.

The subsequent chapters depict a kaleidoscope of transatlantic voyages in first, cabin and tourist classes aboard liners flying the British, Dutch, French, German, Italian and Swedish flags. For a true lover of sea travel, shorter journeys can also be memorable occasions, and they were both less expensive and easily worked into one's travels to the Continent. With a year in Paris and another in London, there were opportunities to sample the traditions of Royal Mail in its waning days on a three-day voyage to Iberia and as a contrast, try out the newest style one-class passenger-car ferry back to England.

The celebrated French Line, with whom I developed sea legs, also operated classy, fast passenger packets in the Mediterranean, and to escape the dreary northern winters, I booked steerage from Marseilles to Majorca and return, and sailed first class with my brother to and from Corsica

I decided to become a teacher during a westbound crossing of the *France* in June, 1968, and I then had long and short vacations to fill. I continued to travel by sea, making the third eastbound voyage of the *Queen Elizabeth 2* in June, 1969.

During one spring vacation, I took the Canadian Pacific Railway to Vancouver and boarded a passenger-cargo ship for a week's voyage along the indented British Columbia Coast. That vessel, the *Northland Prince* which had never been out of sight of land, some years later became Curnow Shipping's first Royal Mail Ship *St. Helena,* rescuing the lonely South Atlantic island following the withdrawal of Union-Castle Line service.

The sea journeys in this book begin in the summer of 1958, a few months before regular jet air travel would arrive and ultimately doom most of the ocean options, and they wind up in 1969 with a two-ship passage aboard Adriatica's pretty little *San Marco* from Istanbul and a connection across the pier in Trieste to the Italian Line's handsome *Cristoforo Colombo* for New York.

With any luck, the story may continue in a subsequent volume with voyages across the Pacific, in the Indian Ocean and back home via the Cape and Suez.

New York, 1998

The *Constitution* embarking passengers at the south side of Pier 84, July 1962. *Richard Sandstrom.*

From the Album: Famous Liners

Above: **The record-breaking Cunarder *Queen Mary*, one of the most popular ships ever to ply the Atlantic, undergoing restoration in 1947 after her war service.** *Arthur J. Ferguson.*

Opposite: **The *Queen Elizabeth*, for many years the largest ship in the World, reverses in the Hudson on the 30th September, 1952 as passengers aboard the French liner *Liberté* look on.** *Arthur J. Ferguson.*

Below: **The *America*, forerunner of the Blue Riband champion *United States*, but herself a very notable liner, seen at Le Havre in May, 1964.** *Theodore W. Scull.*

Top: **The motorship *Vulcania*, noted for her magnificent first class accommodations, preparing to leave New York on her final Italian Line voyage, 21st April, 1965.**
Author's Collection.

Centre right: **Home Lines' *Homeric*, which made one of the most successful transitions from liner to cruise ship, backing into the East River, New York on the 17th May, 1969.**
Theodore W. Scull.

Above: **The beautiful *Nieuw Amsterdam*, pride of the Dutch, entering Southampton, 2nd July, 1969.** *Theodore W. Scull.*

Opposite: **The Italian superliner *Michelangelo* displaying the massive damage to bow and superstructure which she suffered during an Atlantic storm in April, 1966. Two passengers and one crew member were killed.** *Theodore W. Scull.*

Chapter One

Going in Style

THE FRENCH LINE'S *SS LIBERTÉ* AND *SS FLANDRE*

THE FRENCH LINE'S *SS LIBERTÉ*

New York-Southampton, July 1958

1958 seems ages ago, and while the French Line and nearly all the big liners have long gone, that summer proved to be the beginning of a long and happy relationship with England, Europe and travelling by sea. Subsequent travels have only added to a world that was opened on 25th July, 1958.

My Mother chose the line with the help of her great friend whom I had nicknamed "Lady Jane" some years before. She was not actually titled but she had all the good manners to have earned it, and most everyone began to refer to her in this way. She loved the French Line and had very good connections which she used on our behalf. No better choice could have been made.

Pop drove Mother, my brother Sandy and me over to New York in the 1956 Ford station wagon, and this time, instead of passing by the piers en route to Nantucket, we left the elevated West Side Highway and continued a few blocks north to Pier 88, West 48th Street. As we got out of the car, the bow of the *Liberté* loomed overhead, and a tangle of lines, sagging nets and gangways zigzagged across the gap between the ship and the pier.

We handed our cabin luggage over to a longshoreman. It was duly festooned with red, white and blue stickers that read "LIBERTÉ" in white capitals, "French Line" in black script, and in a careful hand on the lines below, our names, cabin number, sailing date and final destination. Colourful French Line tags were securely tied to the suitcase grips. An Oil Market Garage attendant took the station wagon to a nearby lot for Pop to retrieve later.

Embarkation was a bustling affair, but in spite of all the commotion, everything seemed to happen according

The French Line's 51,839-ton *Liberté* at speed on the North Atlantic. Before the War she had been the German record-breaker *Europa*. *Author's Collection.*

The *Liberté*, reverses in the Hudson River. Note her tall pre-War masts. *Arthur J. Ferguson.*

to a plan. Boarding via the first-class gangway, we confronted a line of cabin boys standing at attention in the main entrance foyer. One escorted my Mother to the Chief Purser who introduced himself and told her that there had been a switch in cabins. Instead of sharing with us, she would be sailing in a separate two-bedded outside cabin on the same deck, not far from her two sons.

Two cabin boys then took us separately to our respective accommodations. Our inside cabin No. 85 on Main Deck was quite hot and the punkah louvre ventilation was not having much luck in fighting the July heat wave. It took about 24 hours for the cabin to cool down. Two beds were off to the left with a desk, table and chair in between and closets and chests of drawers along the far wall. But it was the old-fashioned bathroom that drew my attention. The huge tub had five porcelain taps, two marked for hot and cold fresh water, two marked salt and a single one for the fresh water shower.

We left our hand luggage on the beds and went along the linoleum-covered corridors to Mother's cabin, far more cheerful than ours, and with two portholes. Several bouquets of flowers, with little white envelopes attached, were arranged around the cabin. A stack of yellow Western Union Bon Voyage envelopes sat on the desk, and a bottle of Champagne draped with a white linen cloth sat in a silver ice bucket that rested invitingly on the coffee table. Mother had already opened an invitation from the captain to dine at his table, with a note saying that we would be sitting at an adjacent table, presumably so she could keep an eye on us.

Sandy and I were anxious to explore, and we were granted a half hour. The passages were busy with other arriving passengers, cabin boys delivering bon voyage baskets and flowers, and stewards maneuvering baggage trolleys. An expansive glass-enclosed promenade deck ran the length of both sides of the ship. Lines of wooden deck chairs were set up except where the baggage was coming aboard and being stacked for delivery to the cabins. The Grand Salon was the most spectacular place with huge columns soaring up two decks and palm trees flanking an orchestra playing dance music to a few souls seated in almost splendid isolation. Aft along a gallery was a two-deck high library and forward a handsome smoking room, a tiny private bar and a winter garden arcing behind forward facing windows.

Knowing that Pop would be nervous and anxious to get on his way, we returned to Mother's cabin, then went on all the way forward on the Boat Deck to bid him farewell. The blast of the whistle took my breath away. It was designed to be heard for over 20 miles at sea, and we were within a hundred feet or so. Backing into the river started very slowly with a tiny cluster of Moran tugs giving a push. Sagging coloured streamers which had been handed out by the stewards tightened then broke their tenuous connections to the green pier shed. At the far end of the pier, the observation deck was packed, and above the crowd was affixed a large French Line sign. We knew that Pop would not be there, instead already well on his way to beat the crowd.

The *Liberté* was swept sideways by the current, and it was not until opposite Pier 86 that her bow began to turn downriver. High pitched whistles shrieked from the tugs, and we boomed a reply. Progress was slow, but with the ship's deep draught, any speed might send the four screws chopping through the roof of the Holland Tunnel. Once through the Narrows, there was an amazing change of atmosphere on board. All the chaos and hoopla died away, and a calm settled over the decks. And the ship began to roll.

The *Liberté*, launched in 1928 as the *Europa* for North German Lloyd, did not have stabilisers. She was delayed in her delivery by almost a year because of a fire at Blohm & Voss, but when she did enter service in March 1930, she took the Blue Riband on her maiden voyage, averaging 27.9 knots between Cherbourg and Ambrose. While her running mate the *Bremen* became a war loss, the *Europa* survived and was handed over to the French government which allocated her to the French Line. During a winter storm at Le Havre in December 1946, she broke lose, struck the wreck of the French liner *Paris* and sank. Finally, after $16 million had been spent refitting her, and

The *Liberté's* broad Promenade *Charles N. Dragonette Collection.*

after another fire, she re-entered service in August, 1950 as the *Liberté*. At the time of my crossing, she was running with the 1927-built *Ile de France* and the 1952-built *Flandre*. The *Liberté* was no longer so fast as built but she could still manage a respectable 24 knots.

Before dinner, the cabin steward came by to ask what evening clothes we would like to wear. Then after dinner, Sandy and I would return to find our dressing gowns laid out on the turned down beds and the pajamas arranged on the pillow. Then, as on the *QE2's* crossings today, you did not dress on the first or last night out. And something peculiar to Philadelphians, most likely a Quaker thing, we did not dress on Sundays, so Philadelphians could readily recognize one another.

Mother had already found her Philadelphian, a doctor from Paoli, the last suburban station on the Pennsylvania Railroad's Main Line. Dr. Wade, who had been seen off by his family, and Mother became a couple, and together we went for drinks in the main lounge.

Being a teenager, and with all that went along with that age, I was well aware of having to make an entrance into the main dining room. The French Line was famous for its first-class grande descente that put arriving diners in full view of every one already seated. It was a little easier escorting Mother than arriving on my own.

Our table was under the high-ceiling centre section, and the food was more complicated than anything I had experienced, although we ate pretty well at home. The steward was always helpful with something like, "Perhaps the young gentlemen would like to try le canard à l'orange tonight," then translate the entrée with an explanation. Luckily we had been taught a little table French by our grandmother and to like almost everything, so we really enjoyed ourselves. We had caviar every night as a first course and adored watching the flames from the cherries jubilee or crêpes suzettes blaze up from the trolley.

After dinner, we adjourned to the main lounge where a very large orchestra played dance music while we glided around a floor of lighted coloured-glass squares. On the first evening, the girls were seated with their parents around the perimeter, and I met Libby Fowlkes from St. Louis travelling with a girl friend and her parents. She knew everyone we knew from St. Louis who summered on Nantucket including, of course, "Lady Jane."

When the ballroom dancing began to wind down and the older people went off to bed, the evening continued in the Café de l'Atlantique high up on the Sun Deck until the wee hours.

As I got to know a circle of friends, we began to explore the lower classes on our own. Generally, cabin class was not much fun, but tourist class was always lively. We remained in our evening clothes and danced and drank the night away until their lounge and bar shut down. It was usually the floor waxers who shooed us out on deck where we greeted the dawn. The night out came officially to an end, and the next day began about noon.

When I wanted to be alone, I went up to the highest deck in the area around the funnels and dog kennels. At night at sea the illuminated *Liberté* sign was turned off early because there was no one to see it. The few lights around the deck were not so bright and did not take away from the majesty of the clear night sky. Above the huge funnels spewed what appeared to be white smoke at night though it was actually quite dark during the day. The roar of the engines came up through the ventilators, and the wind whipped through the guide wires and mast. There was a feeling of tremendous power underfoot that ceaselessly propelled us forward day after day.

The crossing was smooth and the weather as fine as the North Atlantic could ever be. I enjoyed sitting in a deck chair under lap robes, being served bouillon in the morning and tea and pastries from a trolley in the afternoon. There were deck games to play, and I was pretty good at table tennis.

The French Line did everything in a stylish way, and organising a table tennis tournament was no exception. According to the ship's programme, L'Atlantique, interested players were to gather on the Sun Deck at 10:30 a.m. With our names and cabin numbers on the game plan, we began our matches, and after playing two out of three games, reported the final scores, and were then given the scheduled time for the next round. On it went until I was matched in the finals against a boy named Clark, two years my junior, from Binghamton, New York.

Trying not to make too many excuses, he was a very good athlete, from an athletic family who were also entered in the women's singles and mixed doubles finals. The purser instructed us to wear shorts, sneakers and socks, and the finals were duly announced in L'Atlantique.

We arrived to find over a hundred chairs set up, and as we began our practice, four elevator attendants appeared to serve as ball boys, two at either end. The purser stood by the net as score keeper, and play began. It was all over very quickly, and Clark beat me in straight games and received a silver cocktail shaker embossed with the *Liberté*'s eastbound voyage number New York to Le Havre and the crossing dates, and he didn't even drink. I have forgotten what my present might have been, but it couldn't have been too much, otherwise I would still have it, as I throw out almost nothing. Clark's mother won the ladies' singles and mother and son won the mixed doubles.

After dinner on the gala night, the French Line issued each table a couple of clear plastic bags containing white paper balls about twice the size of a very large marble. The object was toss them all over the room, preferably at friends or someone you wanted to attract. The boys, of course, would dip them in the Champagne glasses, so they would travel farther. The idea was not to wing them as hard as you could, that was frowned upon, but to arc them across the lounge hoping to strike a particular distant target. The whole evening was wonderfully festive, but what a mess for the stewards to clean up.

We still had one night before Southampton, and I got hold of a half dozen of the little bags, then bribed Dr. Wade's cabin steward with one dollar to unlock the door of his single cabin. The steward stood watching as Sandy and I put paper balls into every cavity we could find, in the pockets of his sport jackets, shirt pockets, socks, and shoes. I think that he must have loved the attention, because everybody seemed to know about it, although Mother thought maybe we had taken it too far. That Christmas, he sent us a card saying that he had found another nest of those damn balls in a sports jacket that he had not put on since the summer.

Little fishing boats appeared off the coast of Ireland, and ships came into view as the sea lanes merged off Land's End. Because of the relatively small number of passengers leaving at Southampton, we disembarked into a tender in the Solent. As we pulled away, the *Liberté*'s immense size was once again apparent, as it had been at first sight in New York. Before we had gone very far, the ship's propellers began turning, and the great liner slowly headed away towards the coast of France.

An inside cabin for two.
Alan Zamchick Collection.

The *Liberté's* stylish chapel.
Alan Zamchick Collection.

Top: **The *Liberté's* Library** *Charles N. Dragonette Collection.*

Above: **The Garage, complete with sleek American automobiles.** *Charles N. Dragonette Collection.*

The ride up the Solent and Southampton Water was cramped and most people sat or stood in silence. As we approached the port I could see a magnificent line of ocean liners in unfamiliar colours, with hulls that were not black but white, green and lavender.

Arriving off the Ocean Terminal, we clambered up onto the pier and walked through the huge baggage hall to one of the two boat trains. The passenger carriages were green and the black engine was steam, but it was the sight of the tiny freight wagons that made me laugh. We had booked a Pullman compartment, one with four upholstered highback chairs and a table in between. It was very grand, and we ordered drinks and sandwiches.

Outside the window, steam engines hissed close by and sped past as we made our way up to London Waterloo. At Waterloo, the buffers were lined with steam engines, and we waited for the porters to unload the luggage vans and place the bags under specific letters arranged the length of the curved station forecourt. The taxi queue seemed endless but the dispatching was so well organised that we were soon in the roomiest cab I had ever seen, even larger than the old limousines we had in

New York. The luggage got piled up next to the driver, and soon we were winding through the streets of London en route to Claridge's.

We stayed in London for four wonderful days, then took the Night Ferry via Dover/Dunkerque for a few days in Paris, followed by an overnight Wagon Lit to Interlaken, and a day train to Baden Baden where we took delivery of a snappy black Mercedes 220S coupe. Mother and I sharing the driving, we followed the Rhine into Holland and skirted the north end of the Zuider Zee onto Amsterdam. Taking a trolley from The Hague to the model town of Madurodam, I remember the featured ocean liner being Royal Rotterdam Lloyd's *Willem Ruys*. The S.S. *Rotterdam* was still a year away, then it became the most important ship model.

We toured the World's Fair in Brussels and then drove across Flanders, arriving at Le Havre's Gare Maritime on the day before sailing to have the Mercedes' undercarriage cleaned of possible potato worms that might otherwise migrate to the US. There was no attempt to actually wash the car, so it looked as grubby as ever while we saw it being hoisted on board.

THE FRENCH LINE'S *SS FLANDRE*

Le Havre - New York, August 1958

Mother took one look at the *Flandre* and began to worry out loud about the small size, in spite of its hugely impressive flared bow. Built in 1952 and intended for West Indies service, the *Flandre* was just over 20,000grt while the *Liberté* had been almost 52,000 tons. The *Flandre* had a sister, the *Antilles*, which sported a white hull and carried the originally designed three classes, while the *Flandre* had a traditional black hull and offered just two classes with 200 in first and 500 in tourist.

Le Havre had been badly bombed during the War and it was a dreary place but we had only a night to stay before embarking, arriving at the pier before the boat train arrived from Paris.

Again, we had been upgraded, this time to the Dunkerque Suite, one of two named suites on the Boat Deck. The bedroom had two parallel beds, a writing table and a large window looking out to starboard. The sitting

The 20,469-ton *Flandre* may have been much smaller than her running-mates on the North Atlantic, the *Ile de France* and the *Liberté*, but she was a very stylish, very French ship. *Author's Collection.*

room, where Mother would sleep, had a sofa bed, several chairs and three curved windows looking to starboard and aft over the swimming pool one deck below.

We sailed across the Channel to Southampton to pick up more passengers, then headed out directly into the teeth of an Atlantic gale. It was the kind of storm where the seas were far higher than a Force 6 would warrant. The really strong winds were elsewhere but we took plenty of waves over the bow. My brother took to his bed and remained there for the twelve-hour duration of the storm.

When the storm abated, the social life turned out to be just as gay as coming over, and there were a number of people we knew from Philadelphia. Mother was again seated at the captain's table, and two people that I recall seated there were Regina Resnick, one of the reigning divas of the Metropolitan Opera in New York, and a very high official of the United Nations. Mother said that he appeared so over-awed by Miss Resnick that he was almost afraid to speak.

On the second to last night before New York, there were rumors of a hurricane coming up the East Coast. I hoped that there would be one as the gale had been a wonderful taste of what it could be like in a real storm. When more information was not forthcoming, I decided to do some inquiring myself. I found my way forward and out onto the large open deck ahead of the superstructure. Looking back up to the bridge I fully expected to hear a voice instructing me to return immediately to the passenger accommodation. When that did not happen, I kept going, picking my way around the ropes, cables, winches and cargo hold to the very bow. By now my face was covered in a damp sweat. The temperature, previously in the sixties, had climbed at least ten degrees, and while we were probably in the Gulf Stream, the air was far muggier than coming over. The sea was absolutely calm and the closeness of the air took my breath away. Off to starboard, I could see the Cunard White Star liner *Britannic* with her unmistakable squat funnels, and she appeared to be angling southwest across our bow.

The *Flandre* dives into a trough during hurricane Daisy during the author's westbound crossing, August 1958.
French Line.

A close-up shot of the *Flandre's* exceptionally low, streamlined funnel. *Laurence Dunn Collection.*

The *Flandre's* First Class Dining Room. *Charles N. Dragonette Collection.*

A sailor stood at the bow looking ahead, and he nodded to me when I approached. Using my school boy French, I said something about it being quite hot and wondered if that indicated there might be a lot of wind soon. He replied that a cyclone was coming and would reach us this evening. Suddenly I was quite excited and rushed back to tell Mother and Sandy, who took the news rather badly as he was just beginning to have a good time and had found a girlfriend.

That evening was the gala and everyone was dressed to the nines. Sandy and I went to the dining room early to watch all the people descend the grand staircase. Soon Mother arrived with the captain and his party. At dessert, a messenger arrived and handed the captain a note on a tray. While he read it, everyone at the table stopped talking, and soon he excused himself and left the dining room. I think that everybody had their eyes on him, and conversation dropped noticeably for a few seconds then resumed with even greater intensity.

I now noticed that the ship was moving. Mother came over to our table, and we all left together. Out on the promenade deck, the air was sultry, and through one of the open windows, I could see white caps where the ship's lights illuminated the sea. Little bits of spray blew off the wave tops.

In the ballroom, the captain's place had been taken by another officer and Mother rejoined her table. Dancing with my friend Becky Reath was becoming difficult, for the lighted dance floor was quite slippery and the movement of the ship uneven. Every once in a while, the ship would lurch and send everyone sliding downhill, coming to an abrupt stop where the glass met the carpet. Soon dancing was no longer safe, and we stopped altogether.

In the passageways, the ropes were up and they were especially helpful crossing large foyers. The chairs in the public rooms had already been screwed down, and the shop windows and display cases had been boarded up. Under foot, one moment would be quiet and then came a heavy grinding sound as the stern and props rose and fell.

I returned to the cabin to find Mother in bed and looking not very happy. The ship's movement could be felt even more here being high up and well aft. Sandy was quite sick, and there was nothing for me to do but climb

The First Class Bar on the *Flandre*. *Charles N. Dragonette Collection.*

between the sheets, and with the help of extra pillows from the closet, prop myself against the wall. The beds ran with the ship, and the pitching sent unpleasant pressures through my head.

I slept fitfully until Robert, the steward, came in to see how we were getting on and bearing juice and tea. Sandy was too sick to move, and Mother was white as a sheet. She was frightened enough to ask Robert if we were going to make it. Robert responded that she need not worry because this is a big ship. Mother shot back that the *Flandre* had broken down on her maiden voyage, and Robert said that he had been through many storms on this ship and others. He continued that there would be no breakfast served in the dining room, and that he would bring in some sandwiches later as there might not be any lunch served either. He suggested that we stay in our cabin, or if we wished, he would take us to the more centrally located library.

By now the props were coming right out of the water giving off unpleasant whirring sounds, followed by severe shifting as the ship lost its way and hit the next wall of water. Mother said that it felt like being in an earthquake which she had experienced twice in mild forms.

Mother wanted to stay put and when Robert left, I went exploring, picking, my way along the corridors, making only a few feet at a time. When there was a flat bit, I made a few yards. I felt very much alone in the hallways and found the promenade deck doors locked. The waves were cresting about the height of the deck and the tops came right up against the windows. A steward came along to say that two windows had been broken on the starboard side.

I continued forward to a door that opened onto a sheltered deck which had a set of stairs leading up two decks to the Boat Deck. There just beneath the overhanging bridge, I had a window which allowed me to see both forward and aft along the Boat Deck and up into the rigging and funnel.

Holding onto the railing, I watched the bow drop into a trough, take on a huge wave which would become a wide wall of water crashing directly against the superstructure. The spray that cleared the bridge went back over the ship at times obscuring my view aft. The ship would shift about for a few seconds then the bow would rise to a point where I was looking up at the sky and could no longer see the horizon.

As I looked closely, I saw that the plates extending up past the level of the deck on the starboard side had been bent back. A huge section had given way. I remained for about two hours, still jumping back each time a particularly strong wall of water thundered against the superstructure. Getting hungry, I returned to the cabin and found Mother seated there gritting her teeth. Sandy lay motionless in the bed, and Mother said he had hardly moved all morning. During my absence, a sailor had been thrown into the empty pool during one of the ship's nasty plunges and had been badly hurt.

Robert had seen me pass and he brought some sandwiches. He said that the hospital was full of people who had been hurt, and that hundreds of pieces of crockery had been broken. We were doing only six to eight knots so we would be many hours late arriving in New York.

By early afternoon, the seas abated and at five it was announced that the dining room would reopen. With Robert in charge of Sandy, who still looked awful, Mother and I went down to a virtually empty room. The tables all had special steel contraptions to keep the glasses, dishes and tableware in place. Everything, even the salt and pepper shakers and the wine bottle, had their secure place on the table. We happily ate the first hot meal in 24 hours, though sparingly.

By nine o'clock, the sea was quiet again, the air fresh and the stars blazing from the heavens. I stayed above to get as much fresh air as I could. Because we had sailed a couple of hundred miles off course to try to avoid the worst of the storm, which I do not think that we succeeded in doing, our arrival was set for late in the afternoon, about 10 hours behind schedule.

Lots of people were on hand on the pier. After disembarking, Pop asked first if the car was damaged, but we had no idea, and it was not until it came off in a sling three hours later that we could see that there was not a nick, just the same dirty car.

On the way home, I realized that I would have no problem finding a subject for the first composition of the school year.

The *Flandre* shows off her distinctive profile. *Laurence Dunn Collection.*

Chapter Two

National Flags - Five Crossings

TSS Bremen, MS Kungsholm, TSS Hanseatic, RMS Sylvania

NORDDEUTSCHER LLOYD'S *TSS BREMEN*

New York-Bremerhaven June 1960

Our family trip to Europe in the summer of 1958 had been a great success, and my Father wanted to get in on the fun, so this second time it would be the four of us. I was not yet in on the choice of ships, but as we were travelling to Germany then Scandinavia, North German Lloyd was a natural choice. My Father liked to get there, the faster the better, but not on an American ship so the *United States* was never considered. Instead we booked on the next fastest, the *Bremen.*

Completed in 1939 as the French liner *Pasteur*, the War intervened and she never entered commercial passenger service until July 1959 when she appeared as the 32,336-ton *Bremen.* She became the 23-knot flagship of the revived North German Lloyd, with accommodations for just over 1,100, including 200-plus in first. In effect, we were sailing on a ship less than a year old and that also appealed to Pop.

In those days, North German Lloyd had midnight sailings, and our departure time was 0:01 a.m., one minute after midnight, on 21st June 1960. It was the date that stuck in my parents' mind, but as I was pouring over the brochures the morning of the 19th June, I realised that embarkation was tomorrow evening. I distinctly remember Mother's first reaction, "I haven't had my hair done." Needless to say, there was much to do and Pop, not an easy-going traveller at the best of times, was in a state of agitation, and I knew to stay at a safe distance but be ready to respond if needed.

As a footnote, to avoid this kind of confusion, NGL later moved the sailing time forward two minutes to 11:59

Midnight sailings, or more precisely one minute after midnight, were a tradition with North German Lloyd, and they provided festive embarkations. Passengers and visitors aboard the *Bremen* would be enjoying German beer and dancing to an oompah-pah band. *Author's Collection.*

Showing off her huge funnel, the North German Lloyd liner *Bremen* is outbound for the West Indies on 7th June, 1969. Home Lines' *Oceanic*, also outbound, can be seen in the distance to the right. *Theodore W. Scull.*

p.m. so the embarkation date and sailing date would be the same. The former system was a clever way of making the voyage seem a day shorter. By departing at 0:01 a.m. on 21st June and arriving Bremerhaven on 28th June, it appeared to be a seven-day voyage, while sailing at 11:59 p.m. on 20th, it seemed to be eight days, and in fact it was eight nights.

Of course, we managed to make the sailing though not without a lot of heated arguing about who was going to do what - changing the parlor car seats to New York, cocktails with one group, dinner with another, and advancing the invitations to the Bon Voyage Party, which started at 8:30 p.m. Everyone we knew in New York would want to attend.

My parents had the party in first-class Cabin 185, and we could retreat to ours, 196, when theirs got too crowded. At 11:30 p.m. it was "All Ashore" and the brass band came out on the Promenade Deck playing to the crowd aboard and on the pier. At precisely one minute after midnight we sailed, backing into the North River on a magically clear night.

First class was very formal and staid, and Germans outnumbered Americans two to one. It appeared to be an older crowd than aboard the *Liberté*, but as always, there were several Philadelphia families on board that my parents knew or knew of, and two of them had kids about our age.

On the first evening at sea, Sandy and I returned to our cabin to find our evening clothes laid out on the bed in preparation for the captain's party. The menu was every bit as good as the French Line, and the service was as professional and precise as I have ever experienced. The NGL crossed anchor and key logo on the soup cup, its plate and the service plate were perfectly lined up when put before you. There was no turning it after being set down. One of the stewards told me that the head waiter would take a string and run it down the middle of a line of tables for the full length of the restaurant to make sure that every piece of china and tableware was perfectly placed.

Steak Tartar was on the menu at lunch one day as a special order, and I had never seen such a performance with the steward mixing oil, raw egg, herbs, peppers, onions and whatever else into raw hamburger. It was such theater that I had to try it, but my Father turned up his nose, as he loved to do, and ordered an American Steak à la Minute, medium rare.

The band began precisely at 9 o'clock in the Main Lounge and would wind up on the stroke of midnight, playing mostly German waltzes and the Cha Cha, which the South American Germans loved. Then it was down to E-Deck and the Tavern where the scene was still sophisticated, but also very lively. My recorded bed times started as early as 2:15 a.m., the first night, and ranged between 3:05 and 4:25, with one recording, as the sun rose, at 7 a.m. I just made lunch on that day.

One night my parents learned that my brother had grown up when they decided to have a nightcap in the Tavern, and I was with them. We took the lift down to E-Deck and there was Sandy at a table for two next to the dance floor engaged in an intense conversation and sipping gin and tonic with a beautiful Danish girl. Pop said to my Mother, "Sunny, let's go to bed," and we left and not a word was said until years later when he was in a reminiscing mood after a few nightcaps. "I will never forget the night that your Mother and I...."

On 23rd June while I was watching *Seven Thieves* in the cinema, an announcement came that we would be passing the company's *Berlin* (the former *Gripsholm* of 1925) in about five minutes. What a to-do! The band appeared on deck playing a marching song and along came this dowdy little twin-funneled ship listing to one side as all their passengers and the band were out on deck staring at us. Whistles, music, cheering and in minutes the excitement was all over. The cinema went dark and the film came back on.

We docked at Cherbourg at 7 a.m. on 27th June and lost some friends to the steam-powered boat train for Paris and with German precision we were underway again at eight. The *Bremen* crossed the Channel and set passengers off in a tender in the Solent rather than sail all the way up to Southampton Docks, and we were away at 1:10 p.m. overnight to Bremerhaven.

Off the port with a strong wind blowing, the tugs had much difficulty turning the ship around to berth at Columbus Pier, where a huge crowd was on hand awaiting friends and relations. We were met by a Mercedes and driver and transferred to the Columbus Hotel in Bremen overlooking the main railway station. I had a hard time leaving the window as below there were more steam engines on the move than I had ever seen in my life. Our stretch of the Pennsylvania Railroad back home was all-electric and had been since the 1930s.

In this postcard view North German Lloyd's inbound *Bremen* in the foreground passes the Europe-bound *Berlin* in the Hudson River in the 1960s. *North German Lloyd.*

LIFE ON THE *BREMEN*

Top: **The Scull family in the Veranda Deck Observation Lounge.** *Author's Collection.*

Centre: **Midnight buffet, with the author wearing a fancy dress hat.** *Author's Collection.*

Bottom left: **Teddy and Sunny: The author and his Mother enjoy fine North Atlantic weather.** *Author's Collection.*

Below: **A transatlantic crossing provides a good opportunity to make friends, as the author's brother discovered.** *Author's Collection.*

SWEDISH AMERICAN LINE'S *MS KUNGSHOLM*
Bremerhaven-New York August/September, 1960

It took me just three days to decide that I wanted to return by sea and not by air, so I set out to make inquiries first at the Cunard office in Hamburg, then in Copenhagen where we stayed at the D'Angleterre for six nights. Holland America's *Ryndam*, Home Lines' *Homeric* and Swedish American's *Kungsholm* were all full, and only the Polish Ocean Lines' *Batory* had space, 10 days to Montreal. The *Kungsholm* was my first choice as the ship was mainly tourist class, and all cabins had private facilities, portholes and air-conditioning.

Several days after my first inquiry, the Swedish American Line called the hotel and got my Father's room, and as he had no inkling of my plans, he was none too pleased. He calmed down when I was able to tell him that the sea passage at $265 was $27 less than the value of my air ticket. The rate was a guarantee of a minimum four-berth, my first experience sharing with strangers and travelling tourist class.

That agreed to, we sailed on the old 1937-built *Kronprins Olav* overnight to Oslo, returning several days later, then drove onto Sweden in a rented car, which meant driving on the left side. After sending my Father home, we flew to Italy, and when my Mother and brother left, I went off to Munich and Berlin returning to Bremen on 23rd August in time for the *Kungsholm*'s sailing the next day.

The 21,141-ton motorship *Kungsholm* making her entry into a hazy New York, escorted by Moran tugs.
Laurence Dunn Collection.

The boat train consisted of two carriages up front behind the steam locomotive that were detached at Bremerhaven for Columbus Pier. We arrived but there was no ship until about noon when about one hundred boarded.

I shared Cabin U67 with a grandfather, father and son from Cleveland, Ohio who turned out to be quite nice and very quiet in the mornings, as I tried to be returning late at night. The cabin was much larger than I had expected with two portholes, two sinks, plenty of luggage space and four wardrobes, dressing table, telephone, private shower and good soundproofing.

My tablemates at second sitting were equally delightful with two Finnish girls, two Swedish American women, one Danish American, and two Americans, one a school principal. After French Line and North German Lloyd first class, the menu was not very exciting, and at dinner, the choice was one soup, a fish or meat entrée and one dessert. Coffee was served on the Verandah Deck. I started things off by buying a bottle of wine which stretched to two, and we had a jolly time every meal.

Many of the passengers were also students travelling to America on scholarships and lots of Swedish Americans, of course, though it was not always obvious which side of the Atlantic they actually called home.

The route took us above Scotland and through the Pentland Firth. The weather was blowy and dreary most of the way, so going out on deck to get air became a chore. Dancing was even more difficult, and when the ship rolled, one simply stopped and we slid a few feet then resumed our steps. It was tiring to have to concentrate so hard, and we mostly sat, talked and listened to the band. Otherwise entertainment was bingo and horse racing in the style of the French Line, throwing the dice and moving wooden horses along a mat. The winnings were pretty meagre.

I liked the layout of the ship with all the tourist class public rooms on one deck but there was no long promenade deck as it was divided between first and tourist. I got invited to tea and played Ping-Pong in first class, which made for a change of scenery. There, wasn't a lot of difference in the public spaces as the ship was also built to make long one-class cruises for a fairly upmarket clientele. The food and service would obviously be of a much higher standard in first class and on cruises, at least one would hope.

We had an engine room visit, and I was impressed how quiet, clean and cool it was. During the bridge visit, one of the passengers asked the captain if he had read "Collision Course", the story of the Swedish American liner *Stockholm* ramming the Italian *Andrea Doria*. The passenger then produced a copy. What bad taste, and what an embarrassing chill fell over the group, all of whom were invited guests. I had read the book, and I could never figure out who was at fault.

On our farewell night, which was one night before the festivities in first class and two nights before New York, the menu was fruit cup, consommé, filet mignon and Bombe à la *Kungsholm*. The captain appeared with a band which played the *Kungsholm* song that started with

"Of all the ships that sail the sea,
The ship for me is the *Kungsholm*,
More than just an ocean liner,
Not a ship that's built is finer,
etc."

Then the lights went out and flaming desserts arrived with more song.

On one afternoon, the band had gotten drunk so that night we had no music. I retired to the deck to listen to the fog horn which sounded almost every minute as we were off the Grand Banks. We were not moving very fast but I overheard that we were 15 hours ahead of schedule thus allowing us to make this cautious speed and still be able to arrive on time in New York. It was quite spooky as occasionally one heard other whistles and horns. Some seemed not far off, and there was a lot of course changing. The next morning the fog was even thicker and we came to a complete stop twice.

The last night at dinner was a riot, and the two Finnish girls first pinned a flower on my lapel then gave me a homemade diploma for satisfactory completion of my Finnish lessons, which consisted of learning about a dozen words that I still remember nearly four decades later. I cannot say that my vocabulary has increased as it is an impossible language and bears no resemblance to anything else with which I am even remotely familiar. The table of almost teetotalers started off by ordering very dry Martinis, then wine, and Champagne and everyone ended up quite flushed. The fun and laughter got carried to the lounge for some folk dancing.

On 1st September, it was foggy, warm and humid when the *Kungsholm* made her way up river to Pier 97 passing the docked *United States*, *America*, an Italian liner that I did not record and the *Mauretania*. Mother met me on the pier, and as the Pennsylvania Railroad was on strike, we drove home in the Buick. It had been quite a summer, especially the part where I was on my own. It set the stage for more travels abroad.

HAMBURG-ATLANTIC'S *TSS HANSEATIC*
New York-Southampton, June 1961 and August 1963

During the 1961 spring semester, my university French professor convinced me to advance my studies at the Université de Neuchatel in Switzerland, so I had a good excuse to sail again. There was a whole world of transatlantic shipping from which to choose, and I set my sights on those with large tourist classes rather than ships with first, cabin and tourist which would mean travelling in the bottom of the three. Newer ships would be around for some time, so something older and full of character suited best. It came down to the 30,000-ton *Hanseatic*, and the schedule worked.

Hamburg-Atlantik Linie
TS „HANSEATIC"
TOURIST CLASS
BAGGAGE ROOM

Built in 1930 as the *Empress of Japan*, she had been the largest and fastest liner on the Pacific before the War, and after a half-dozen years on the Atlantic as Canadian Pacific's *Empress of Scotland*, she was bought and refitted in a joint venture between the City of Hamburg and the Home Lines. By 1961 she had been sailing as the *Hanseatic* for Hamburg-Atlantic for three years, now sporting two funnels and a completely different passenger mix with only 85 passengers in first class and almost 1,200 in tourist.

Paying a fare of $242, I had Main Deck cabin number 27, a four-berth with private shower. Travelling over with a friend from boarding school, our respective parents took us to dinner at the same restaurant then to Pier 97. The bon voyage party included friends from both school and college. One Champagne bottle must have gotten well shaken up on the way over to 12th Avenue, as almost half its contents emptied out when the cork popped.

Like the *Bremen*, the ship was scheduled to sail at 12:01 a.m. on 11th June but there was no last minute confusion about boarding the evening before. It was a grand departure and the two of us stayed up well past the Statue of Liberty.

I had three German cabin mates, and two of them

A midnight view of the *Hanseatic* at Southampton. *Laurence Dunn Collection.*

yelled at each other during the night, so I had little enough rest to face the first day at sea. Happily they had first sitting, so I could sleep in and get dressed without jockeying for position in the relatively tight quarters. The cabin was a Bibby-type, L-shaped with a narrow corridor that led to the wash basin and porthole.

My school friend and I shared the table with a Canadian couple from Hamilton, Ontario on their way to England for 15 months, then out to New Zealand to live. I never did find out the reason for the long stopover, but they were very pleasant and slowly warmed up to being quite a lot of fun. The dining room was quite splendid with a double-height ceiling in the centre and an orchestra balcony, but our table was located under the low-ceiling section on the port side. I enjoyed the food much better than the *Kungsholm*, which had less choice and was rather bland. One night we had a grand buffet set up outside the restaurant, but there was so much to choose from, it took a half-hour of queuing before getting to the table.

The *Hanseatic* prided itself on being almost one class, and one was hardly aware of first above us. We had an entire deck of public rooms and long glass enclosed promenades. The Alster Club, the forward observation bar, had huge nearly floor-to-ceiling windows and heavy curtains that were drawn at night. The bar opened at 10 a.m., and the German beer drinkers populated the place early on. It was extremely attractive before and after dinner, and the music was more modern than the main ballroom. The band often played Latin American and Italian tunes, for listening rather than dancing. Galleries led back to the writing room and library, two main lounges, the Winter Garden and finally the St Pauli Tavern, a noisy, crowded and smoky German pub.

First class with accommodations for 85 was located almost entirely on the Boat Deck. The forward observation lounge, divided into sections, served as the music room, bar and writing room. The all-outside cabins faced onto the Boat Deck and the dining room was all the way aft, not unlike the position of the *Queen Mary's* Verandah Grill with windows looking over the stem, and in the *Hanseatic*'s case, facing the outdoor pool. The indoor swimming pool, gymnasium and massage room, forward on A Deck, had designated hours for the two classes.

The passenger list showed ten pages sailing to Cuxhaven, the port for Hamburg and three each for Southampton and Le Havre. The ship was certainly more German than the *Bremen* but then this was also a middle-class tourist-class crowd. There were lots of females to

The 30,026-ton *Hanseatic* arrives in New York's Upper Bay. Above the ship's bow, a tug bearing the docking pilot approaches and in the background, a United Fruit banana boat is tied up at Pier 3. *Hamburg-Atlantik-Linie.*

The *Hanseatic* at Cuxhaven. *Alan Kittridge collection.*

meet in the evening, many going over for summer studies or travelling through Europe for a couple of months.

The days were foggy, hazy, cloudy and drizzly with some very heavy periods of rain, so we must have been travelling the same speed as a low pressure front. I got outside to throw the medicine ball and play some deck tennis intermittently, but most times the others found it too cold. I enjoyed long walks on the Boat Deck, invariably by myself.

I took the *"Last Voyage of the Lusitania"* out of the library, but I felt quite safe on a German ship. There were lots of good places to read other than the main public rooms, which always seemed crowded as the poor weather kept everyone inside most of the time. The ship did not pitch much but it did roll as she had no stabilisers, shades of the *Liberté*, but more pronounced because of the swells on this voyage. The films alternated between German and English, so I frequented the cinema only every other day.

The evenings were great fun. There was always company and I had no hesitation simply sitting down with a few girls who appeared to be on their own. The only problem came when finding seats for the group if we moved from the main lounge to the St. Pauli Tavern. Often after getting drinks at the bar, we had to move out into the Winter Garden or to the long promenade deck which was invariably empty after dark. There was quite a lot of shifting partners and some girls seemed to have two dates a night, one directly after dinner and another later, but some of this resulted from the two sittings. There were odd times to fill if you enjoyed being with people.

Hamburg-Atlantik Linie

ss HANSEATIC - West Germany Registry

S.S. HANSEATIC

30.029 t

KABINENPLAN

PASSENGER ACCOMMODATION PLAN

Ausgabe 1965 · Edition 1965

The *Hanseatic* was a pretty steady 20-knot ship, and we made from 461 to 475 miles a day and lost an hour on five of the nights which meant arriving in England quite exhausted. There was no going to bed early to compensate, but there was a choice of missing breakfast which happened more often than not. The stewards tended to be very good in not disturbing those who slept in until almost lunch time.

By the last two days at sea, my friend and I had settled with two girls who we then planned to meet in Paris where we were scheduled to join several friends from university. I would be disembarking in Southampton, going up to London for a few days then deciding how I was going to cross the Channel. I did not have to be in Neuchatel until 7th July, so there were nearly three weeks ahead to plan.

The *Hanseatic* docked in Southampton after 9 p.m. on 17th June, and the boat train got me up to London and in a taxi to the Regent Palace by 1:00 a.m. The place was still very busy at this late hour, and I was able to get a single for 39 shillings in a location almost directly on Piccadilly Circus. I had my own room again.

I made my first transatlantic flight home that summer on BOAC from London, which also involved very complex arrangements to bring back a Cavalier King Charles Spaniel from Axminster in Devon to Philadelphia. It was a nightmare of bureaucracy and travel schedules, and the next King Charles came back far more stylishly on the *Nieuw Amsterdam*.

Two years later, in 1963, I had graduated from university and wanted to spend a year abroad. I chose the foreign studies course at La Sorbonne. To help pay for the year, I sold my last car, an Oldsmobile F85 that was less than a year old.

Curiously, I chose the *Hanseatic* again, this time sailing on 12th August just after the summer fares went down. The fare was $235, seven dollars less than I had paid two years before, for a lower berth in U121, an outside cabin quite far aft on Upper Deck.

It was an afternoon sailing, and somewhat nerve-wracking as I would be leaving for a full year and had no idea where I would be living in Paris as there was no choice of student housing. Therefore, I carried sheets, towels, blankets and the like which added to a baggage count of a half-dozen pieces. We had them delivered early to the pier to be placed in the hold, and I would not see them again until after I disembarked.

This voyage was quite similar to the previous one except that the ship was more German, if that could be true. There were ten pages of passengers bound for Cuxhaven and only single pages for Cherbourg and Southampton. Many announcements were not even made in English and the bingo numbers were called out in German only, so one learned some of this language out of necessity.

It was again very social, but there were fewer people from whom to choose as this was an older crowd. This ship had a good long life and might have sailed past 40 had she not had a fire at her New York pier on 7th September 1966, with smoke damage which was too heavy to repair.

CUNARD'S *RMS SYLVANIA*

Liverpool-New York, June/July 1964

In June, 1964, I had come to the end of an almost full year at the Sorbonne in Paris, and I was rapidly running out of money. I hesitated to ask my parents for more, as it was time to come home and find a job. I had a steamship ticket on the Cunarder *Sylvania* sailing from Liverpool on 30th June, the very last day before the westbound fares went up for the summer.

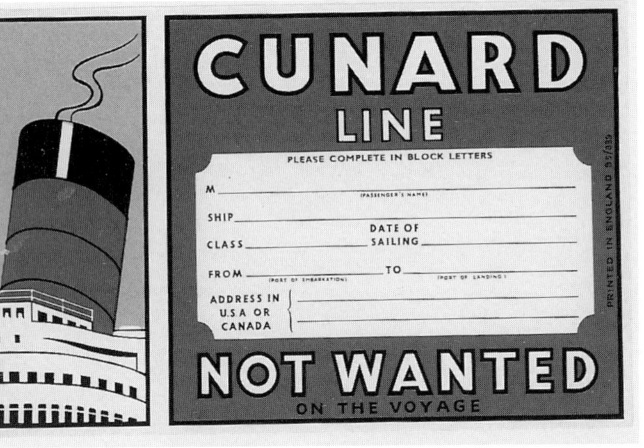

In the meantime, I could work for my keep with friends on a farm in Wiltshire, but I still needed to stretch out the remaining money after they went on holiday, and that left me with four days on my own before sailing.

I travelled up to Liverpool Lime Street via Reading, Oxford and Birmingham. Upon leaving my baggage at the Left Luggage, I spotted arriving passengers with Booth Line labels. The line traded to the coast of Brazil and 850 miles up the Amazon to Manaus. As it was my first visit to Liverpool, and I had no idea how far it was to the Prince's Landing Stage, I set off at a fast clip and arrived at the Pier Head just as the Booth Line's *Hubert* was swinging in the river to make for Birkenhead to unload cargo. I could see an Anchor and a Bibby liner across the Mersey and many funnels in the docks beyond the Landing Stage, so there would be plenty of ships and lines I had never seen before.

I found a bed and breakfast just alongside Lime Street Station that turned out to be a boarding house with an all-male clientele of clerks who came down for breakfast each morning in suits and spoke to no one. I was afraid to even ask for the sugar as that would break the silence, but otherwise, I was well informed of the house rules by the landlady, including when I could take a bath, which was after everyone had left for work. Never mind, I would be out all day, and the price at 11s. 6d was right.

At the Landing Stage, I met someone who told me about the free access to the port with a pass from the Mersey Docks and Harbour Board. The Board's headquarters was the third in line on the waterfront after the majestic Royal Liver Building and the low classical-style Cunard Building.

I filled out a form, including my passport number, and was granted a pass good for one year that included "permission to take Photographs and/or make Sketches on the Dock Estate...". Most of the interesting shipping was in the Brocklebank, Canada, and Gladstone Docks and across the river at Birkenhead. The Mersey ferries left from right in front of the Harbour Board and the Isle of Man steamers docked at the upriver end of the Landing Stage.

I was most captivated by the Blue Funnel liners, *Helenus, Clytoneus* and *Perseus,* docked bow to stern with their handsome bridge fronts, pronounced sheer and tall upright blue and black stacks. Laurence Dunn's first *Passenger Liners* had introduced me to a whole new world of non-transatlantic liners, and Liverpool was the centre, albeit fast winding down with the Empire's demise.

Still, I saw Elder Dempster's *Aureol,* Anchor Line's *Circassia,* New Zealand Shipping's *Remuera* (ex-*Parthia*) and Bibby Line's just laid up *Warwickshire.* Pacific Steam's *Reina del Mar* arrived at the Landing Stage to embark 925 passengers for a voyage to New York, beginning at £60, for Travel Savings Association. On the day I crossed the Mersey, the *Empress of England* moved to the Landing Stage, a handsome white liner set against a signature line of important buildings and a dark forbidding sky. The *Empress of England* would sail as I was standing on the Landing Stage waiting for the *Sylvania* to take her place.

The *Sylvania* was the last of four 22,000-ton sisterships built for St. Lawrence service to Quebec and Montreal. Completed in 1957 by John Brown, Clydebank, she had a smallish first class complement of 150 and 700 in tourist. With the Canadian service in decline, she was placed on the Liverpool-New York route and provided an inexpensive fare of £76.10s.

I was booked into inside cabin A - 15 all the way

Reina del Mar **at the Landing Stage, Liverpool embarking passengers on a £60 cruise to New York chartered by Travel Savings, Ltd., 28th June, 1964.** *Theodore W. Scull.*

Cunard's *Sylvania*, here seen on her trials, was one of four sisters built for the Canadian service, but she was soon transferred to the Liverpool-New York route. *Laurence Dunn Collection.*

Above: **Officially out of bounds to the author, who was travelling Tourist, the First Class smoking room of the *Sylvania* was traditionally furnished, with its wood panelling and red fabrics.**
Vincent Messina Collection.

Cunard
R·M·S
All Cunard Liners are of British Registry
"SYLVANIA"
Plan of
FIRST CLASS
accommodation

A two-berth tourist cabin on *Sylvania's* A-deck, similar to the one in which the author travelled, except that his did not have a porthole.
Vincent Messina Collection.

The Tourist Class smoking room on the *Sylvania* was more contemporary in style.
Vincent Messina Collection.

forward on A Deck, with upper and lower berths, two wardrobes, a dressing table, chair and wash basin. We sailed at 8 p.m. on 30th June, then anchored off Cobh the next morning at 10 o'clock for about four hours, embarking passengers by tender. The boat drill, required within 24 hours of sailing, was held soon after leaving Ireland for the open sea.

My one peek into first class revealed pre- and post-War styles with lots of shades of red covering chairs and sofas and in the carpets, and very cozy rooms that might be found at a genteel country hotel. Tourist class had a main lounge where keep fit classes took place in the morning, afternoon tea at 3:45 p.m., and live music every other day-otherwise it was recorded. There were morning or afternoon dance instructions, a pianist at 8 p.m. for those who ate at the first sitting, bingo (housie housie) every night at nine, except for one night of horse racing, and a cabaret some nights at 11:30.

The smoking room, one deck above and aft, was mostly a bar and very popular, with recorded music every night at 6:30 and a duo playing at seven. The cinema, with a balcony for first class and main level for tourist, showed a different film twice a day on varying schedules and included *Sunday in New York*, *From Russia with Love*, *Mutiny on the Bounty*, and *A Ticklish Affair*.

Happily, my cabin mate trusted me enough to lend some money for drinks and tips, and flush with cash, I began ordering Pimm's No 1 Cup, not exactly the least expensive drink on the bar list. I did the terrible American thing of snapping my fingers for the steward, just once, and he pretended that I did not exist for the rest of the voyage. With the North Atlantic weather overcast every day, there were few outdoor activities, so it was mostly an all-day social hour in the smoking room.

We spent American Independence Day at sea, and the festivities were pretty much limited to a concert entitled "Billy Williams and His Augmented Orchestra" at 3 p.m. in the cinema. This was a British ship, after all, but I was feeling slightly more patriotic after a year abroad.

The Abstract of the Log has us abeam the Ambrose Channel Light Vessel at 0930 hours on 7th July having steamed 2,840 miles at an average speed of 19.93 knots, putting us alongside Pier 90 at Noon.

Within a few weeks, I had landed a first job at Holland America Line in the 609, Fifth Avenue passenger reservations office. Holidays would now be limited to a fortnight.

Chapter Three

The Other French Line

SS Président de Cazalet, SS Ville de Marseille, SS Sampiero Corso

NAVIGATION MIXTE'S
PRÉSIDENT DE CAZALET
Marseilles-Palma de Majorca
and CGT'S *SS VILLE DE MARSEILLE*
Palma-Marseilles, February 1964

Compagnie Générale Transatlantique, sometimes called the French Line or CGT or Transat, was well known for operating all of its far-flung passenger services with great style, whether it be the mighty Atlantic liners, the classy and fast North African packets or the smallish overnight boats to Corsica.

As I have already described, French Line travel came into my life at age seventeen, when with some reluctance, I agreed to go to Europe with my Mother and brother in July 1958, travelling over on the giant *Liberté* and coming home on the much smaller but highly memorable *Flandre*.

Later, in 1963 and 1964, when I spent nine months studying at La Sorbonne in Paris, I had a tiny flat in Montparnasse. Making my weekly mail runs to American Express near Place de l' Opéra, I would pass the French Line booking office just down the street at 6, Rue Auber. In the right front window, the entire French Line fleet, about 40 tiny scale models, was displayed for all to admire. Inside, travellers could book cabin space for New York, the West Indies, the West Coast, islands in the Mediterranean, and several ports along the North African littoral.

Timetable cover with the two companies' funnels.

Messageries Maritimes had a splendid Bd. de la Madeleine office just down the road from the Café de la Paix. The front window exhibited a world map on which were placed little magnets embossed with evocative ships' names: *Cambodge*, *Ferdinand de Lesseps*, *Mekong*, *Tahitien*, etc. The company whose motto was "The world is our oyster" had a large fleet of passenger and cargo-passenger ships, and about midday, a clerk would appear in the window and, using a short pole, move the fleet to new noon-time positions. Inside the booking hall, signs above the desk indicated the different services (en français, bien sûr): Indian Ocean, Asia, the Pacific Ocean and South America.

By the middle of January 1964, the seemingly endless days of drizzle that characterise winter in Paris had me thinking about an unofficial break from school, somewhere that was sunny, inexpensive and reachable by sea. The planning began with a call at the offices of the Compagnie de Navigation Mixte at 1, Rue Scribe. The French Line and Mixte offered a joint weekly service from Marseilles to Palma de Majorca, the main port in Spain's Balearic Islands, not to mention frequent sailings to Algiers, Oran, Bone (Annaba), Skikda (Philippeville) and Tunis in North Africa. France maintained strong economic ties with Algeria even after Algerian independence was declared in July 1962.

Travelling as a student meant booking the cheapest possible accommodations, which on these ships was fourth or deck class for a return fare of 72 NF or about $14 plus a couple of dollars in taxes. Deck class in the month of February, I was told, was 'tween deck, protected from the nasty seas that can be a feature of the Mediterranean in the dead of winter. The idea sounded like a lark.

Setting out with two female friends, one American and one German, we left from the Gare de Lyon by the night train for Marseilles. Sitting bolt upright in a crowded eight-seat compartment was less than comfortable, and the green leatherette seats were firm enough to require regular changes of posture to keep one's circulation going.

After a restless night, we were delighted with the opportunity to walk the short distance from Gare St. Charles down the monumental staircase to the Gare Maritime Joliette. In 1964, apart from North and South Atlantic sailings, Marseilles was France's principal maritime gateway to the rest of the world. Passenger ships belonging to a half-dozen companies offered regular departures to North, East, South and West Africa, to the Indian Ocean, South and Southeast Asia, the Far East, and via Panama to the Pacific Islands and Australasia.

Marseilles had long since outgrown its original Vieux Port with the expansion of the French overseas empire in the 19th century and the opening of the Suez Canal in 1869. Now a long artificial breakwater protected the huge commercial dock area from the Mediterranean Sea. The Gare Maritime Joliette was the busy heart of the short sea passenger trade, and its series of finger piers were similar in arrangement to the liner piers in New York. The packet ships could easily be seen and photographed from the shore, and the activity was constant, with multiple daily

The *Président de Cazalet* at her berth in Marseilles. Post-War Navigation Mixte ships usually had a long, low appearance. *Laurence Dunn Collection.*

departures and arrivals mostly to and from Morocco, Algeria, Tunisia and Corsica.

The *Président de Cazalet* belonging to the Compagnie de Navigation Mixte, looked trim and inviting, tied up alongside her berth. The single black, curved Strombos funnel was marked with two narrow red bands flanking the letters N M over a single broad white band. Completed in 1947 by Swan Hunter, Newcastle, the 5,227-ton *Président de Cazalet* had the pleasant low profile of a traditional semi-fast packet ship.

In the huge transit shed, there was surprisingly little embarkation activity. The steward at the foot of the gangway, speaking in the difficult-to-understand accent of Marseilles, said that there were only 50 passengers booked for today's sailing. The ship could handle over 800 in four classes, including 500 in the lowest class, which in the past might have been soldiers as *militaires* was also written on the plan.

While the ship was Algiers-bound, direct sailings were more popular than ones diverted to Palma de Majorca as the stop added five hours to the voyage. In addition, February was not a busy time of the year for tourists to Majorca or travellers to North Africa.

Our 'tween deck accommodations were reached by walking forward along the narrow promenade deck, then descending a steep flight of stairs into a large open area surrounding the forward cargo hold beneath the foredeck. When the cargo handling was completed, the hatch cover was replaced, cutting off the natural light coming in through the opening. The sensation down below was much like being confined to a dungeon. The vertical bulkhead supports added to the severity of the space, and the upward sloping deck narrowed to a sharp point at the bow. Hundreds of canvas deck chairs were stacked up against the side of the hull, and for a couple of francs, we hired a *chaise pliante* for the duration of the voyage.

My two companions were to be the only females travelling fourth class. The rest of the deck passengers were Algerian male migrant workers whose French I found practically unintelligible and who provided the two girls with a great deal of well-meaning but unwelcome attention. I had my work cut out fending them off without offending them.

The *Président de Cazalet* sailed at 6 p.m., and once beyond the port's protected waters, the ship took on a heavy roll sending everything not tied down crashing to the deck. Rows of unused deck chairs broke loose and slid about until the crew retrieved them and had them securely fastened.

It is generally accepted that eating something light is a good precaution rather than trying to ride out a storm on an empty stomach. The little stand-up bar, placed in one corner of the 'tween deck space, served the ubiquitous ham sandwiches, hard-boiled eggs, soft drinks, coffee and little else. While munching on a sandwich, I listened to the thundering sounds of waves striking the ship's bow,

CGT's *Ville de Marseille*, although a North African packet, had the appearance of an ocean liner.
Laurence Dunn Collection.

followed on closely by spray sweeping the deck overhead. There could be no thought of going above to get some air or to witness the spectacle of angry seas. We were confined below decks for the night, having a brief taste of what millions of migrants experienced for days and weeks on end.

The swaying, rolling and pitching allowed for little sleep for the second night running. However, the reclining deck chair was more restful than the straight-back railway seat had been, and we had lots of space.

Shortly after dawn, the seas calmed and we went above to have a look at the island of Majorca rising out of the seas in a series of low peaks. It took my eyes a few minutes to adjust to the bright day after the long confinement in dim light. Palma's cathedral at the far end of the breakwater was by far the largest of the long line of low buildings arcing around the crescent-shaped waterfront

At this time of the year, with very few visitors on the island, it was not difficult to find a reasonably priced hotel costing under two pounds for lodging and three perfectly acceptable meals. At these prices, we could even afford to have an occasional meal outside the hotel.

While the Mediterranean was too cold for swimming, the clear and relatively warm weather was just the change we sought from gray Paris. Most of the time was passed exploring the town of Palma, watching the elderly Trasmediterránea inter-island fleet load and unload, riding an odd, narrow-gauge railway through almond orchards and hills to the port of Soler on the far side of the island, and consuming a lot of hearty Spanish wines.

On the last day, we dined in a waterfront café and then waited the arrival of the *Ville de Marseille* from Algiers in a small bar on the second floor of the maritime station.

Gazing out to sea from the darkened room, I wasn't sure in which direction to look to spot the approaching ship.

Around midnight, over an hour late, the *Ville de Marseille* appeared quite suddenly from behind a headland. Resembling a small city with lights ablaze, she moved rapidly broadside until just outside the harbour, then veered to port and headed straight for the long pier. The *Ville de Marseille,* with distinctive red and black funnel, was an impressive sight indeed.

The ship's gross tonnage of 9,576 made her almost twice the size of the *Président de Cazalet.* She had been completed in 1951, with her sister the *Ville de Tunis* coming a year later, and the four *Ville* ships, including a pre-War pair, made up the backbone of CGT's North

Some years later on the 10th July, 1969, the 21-knot *Ville de Marseille* wastes no time in getting up speed on a 19-hour voyage from Marseilles to Skikda (formerly Philippeville) in Algeria. *Theodore W. Scull.*

After a stormy overnight crossing from Palma de Majorca to Marseilles on the *Ville de Marseille*, the weather improved. 10th February, 1964. *Theodore W. Scull.*

The traditional enclosed promenade deck of Second Class on the *Ville de Marseille*. *Author's Collection.*

The Second Class Bar Fumoir. *Author's Collection.*

The First Class dining room. *Author's Collection.*

A First Class inside 2-berth cabin. Presumably the vase of flowers was removed before a stormy crossing. *Author's Collection.*

African fleet. Operating at a service speed of 21 knots, they could make the Marseilles-Algiers passage in under 20 hours. Only Navigation Mixte's 1950 *Kairouan* was faster at 24 knots.

About two dozen passengers boarded at Palma on what again appeared to be an almost empty ship. Though the port agent had not been able to accommodate us, we had no difficulty in securing an inexpensive, tourist-class cabin from the purser. Inside berths on B Deck were preferable to spending another night in a canvas chair.

Once clear of the port, the ship began to pitch, then after setting a northeasterly course, she went into a regular roll. The company brochure touted stabilisers but I felt no evidence of their use. Bedded down in a pitch black cabin, I could hear my shoes sliding across the linoleum floor with almost every list. At first I listened in amusement, then thought better of it and put the shoes in a drawer for the night. I wedged myself firmly against the bulkhead, then took in the sounds of the groaning ship and in time went off to sleep.

When fully awake the next morning, I felt a queasiness never experienced before at sea. Thinking about it only made me feel worse. I took a few deep breaths hoping to drive the seasickness away but failed to do so. I could now begin to understand how Charles Darwin must have felt for over a year on his long voyage around South America in the *Beagle*. Thinking about him in this stuffy cabin was only adding to the misery, so I quickly dressed and went above.

The ship was wide open, and the dining room officially closed for the duration of the storm. The steward in charge offered me some bread and an apple and suggested that I find a comfortable chair on the promenade deck and stay there. After a few nibbles of sustenance and some fresh air, my spirits returned. I even enjoyed watching, without moving my eyes, the sky and the sea alternate positions through the promenade deck windows. The ship whipped back and forth in a rapid seesaw motion. When an occasional wave top broke against the glass, a more midships location seemed advisable. I joined my two friends in the first-class lounge, and we sat mostly in silence observing the room rise and fall.

Quite unexpectedly, the *Ville de Marseille* went into a particularly steep roll, and Angelika was pitched out of her chair and sent sliding across the dance floor. Her right foot caught the leg of a loose chair upending it into a showcase of French perfumes and shattering the glass. In the process, she received a nasty cut on her knee, and with the help of a steward, we carried her aft to the doctor's office along the Promenade Deck. He bandaged her and she remained in the hospital until the ship had almost reached Marseilles later in the afternoon.

I did not have the chance to appreciate the ship's fine appointments until we reached calmer seas. The first-class main lounge and restaurant had tasteful décor and comfortable leather furnishings. Both rooms extended out to the side promenades running about half the length of the superstructure. Aft on Boat Deck, the attractive bar and smoking room had a raised ceiling and windows facing the sea on three sides.

Tourist class also had its lounge on Promenade Deck surrounded on three sides by open decks. The restaurant was located below on A Deck with high density seating at long tables. Elliptical wood veneer columns were a feature of every public room.

The arrival at Marseilles was clear and very blowy, and we were quite glad to disembark and have a proper hot meal. Angelika's knee was sore but happily there was no long-term damage. We elected to hitch hike back to Paris and walked to the nearby lorry terminal and in no time found a ride to the end of a Metro line at the edge of the city.

CGT'S *SS SAMPIERO CORSO*

Marseilles-Bastia and Bastia-Nice, March 1964

When in early March, I learned that my brother would be coming to Paris for the Easter recess, I suggested a short side trip to the Mediterranean island of Corsica on the way to meeting our parents and great aunt in Nice.

At the time, Corsica was undeveloped enough to be off the beaten track, especially for the motorist. Four French Line passenger ships maintained a regular, frequent service to Corsican ports from Marseilles and Nice. Of the four, only the 1960-built *Napoléon* had drive-on vehicle capabilities. The other three, the 1925 *Cyrnos*, the 1936 *Sampiero Corso* and the 1948 *Commandant Quère* crane-loaded cars and cargo in the traditional manner. Except for an occasional day sailing from Nice to Calvi and Ile Rousse, all scheduled crossings were classic overnight runs.

I was pleased to be able to go into the French Line's Paris office and book a double first-class cabin aboard the *Sampiero Corso* with dinner for the outward passage from Marseilles to Bastia and return from Bastia to Nice for £23. We set out from Paris in a hired Citroen 2 CV determined to avoid the infamous raceway to the south, National Route 7. Travelling over three-digit byways, we crossed the Massif Central to Vichy and Nîmes and two and a half days later we were having bouillabaisse in a restaurant fitted with portholes overlooking Marseilles' harbour entrance. The highly seasoned fish stew originated here in Provence and, given its consistency, it was easily a meal in itself.

From our cliff-side location, we saw the *Djebel Dira*, one of the slower North African packets, appear over the horizon. Belonging to Navigation Mixte, the days for this small 4,180-ton ship were already numbered. With a limited passenger capacity of less than 200 and a service speed of only 16 knots, the *Djebel Dira* represented an older style of immediate post-War passenger-cargo ship. The two could be mixed but the formula was now becoming the roll-on ferry liner.

We finished lunch and were on the pier to see the ship disembark mostly Algerian passengers. The boarding of our rather dowdy-looking 345-foot *Sampiero Corso* turned out to be not unlike embarking on a great ocean liner for an overseas journey. The passenger shed was alive with loading activity. Porters laden with oversize leather cases led a steady stream of passengers up the sloping gangway. Ahead, stewards in starched white jackets directed new arrivals to the left or right depending on the class

Cie. de Navigation Mixte's 24-knot *Kairouan*, the fastest ship in North African service, seen leaving Gare Maritime Joliette for Algiers on 10th July 1969. *Theodore W. Scull.*

indicated on their tickets. Canvas mail sacks, heavy baggage and automobiles were being hoisted on deck and lowered into the forward hold. The atmosphere was just right for an overnight crossing

Our cabin, not a great deal larger than a railway compartment, was fitted with upper and lower berths. It faced aft onto the open deck where a large party of British school children and their harried chaperones vied for territory with the backpackers. Only a few feet and a single pane of glass separated first class from fourth.

Class barriers were rigorously enforced after the 6 p.m. departure. Tonight was a capacity sailing and the services on this little ship were strained to the limit. In these tight conditions, the line could not have passengers wandering about outside the accommodations for which they paid. And it was a satisfying feeling being on the first class side of the fence for a change.

The French Line had acquired the *Sampiero Corso* from Fraissinet when CGT assumed operation of the Corsican services after the War. Built in 1936, the ship had been seized by the Germans, then scuttled in 1944. After several years of layup in Toulon, the *Sampiero Corso* received a new 140-foot midsection and returned to service in 1951 Her gross tonnage was now 4,041 and her passenger capacity 113 first, 115 third and 596 fourth, actually down from her pre-conversion capacity of 1,000.

The first-class accommodations were arranged on Promenade and A decks. Designed for night service, the ship's range of public rooms was limited to a forward lounge bar and a dining room seating 60 at two sittings. An unusually wide glass-enclosed promenade deck provided additional deck chair seating. The outside cabins faced the open or enclosed promenade decks, and only the deluxe cabins had en suite facilities. First class also had access to the Boat Deck for an open-air walk.

Third class, designated as such on the deck plans, was written as second class in the tariff schedules. The cabins consisted of mainly four-berths and a few two-berths with washbasins; and couchette-style dormitory space arranged around the forward hold and forward on A Deck. The public rooms were a sit-down restaurant and a bar on B Deck.

In true French Line fashion, the tradition of complimentary table wines was carried right down to the Corsican packets. The custom added something special to the excellent cream soup, a herb omelette, charolais beef entrée, cheese and fruit, with after-dinner coffee served in the adjacent smoking room. The printed menu showed a colour cover photograph of the *Ville de Marseille* in the port of Algiers, a ship which was now an old friend of less than a month. Second sitting was a most pleasant affair, sharing the table with two French businessmen en route to a sales meeting in Bastia. Unfortunately, while the sea was a virtual mill pond, a slight roll sent my brother to the open deck before the second course arrived.

After dinner, we met on the promenade deck where passengers seated in deck chairs were talking quietly or watching pairs of strollers taking their constitutionals. Up on the Boat deck, the scene was positively serene. The air was clear and cool, and the calm sea shimmered under the light of the half moon and millions of stars. The reflections of light on the water made it seem that the ship was moving at high speed. But if one looked directly over the side, the leisurely pace was easier to assess.

This company postcard was accidentally printed in reverse, as the name on the *Sampiero Corso*'s bow shows.
Cie. Générale Transatlantique.

While we luxuriated practically alone beneath the life boats, a look aft to the open deck below revealed several hundred shifting forms making themselves comfortable for the night. Under these ideal weather conditions, deck travel appeared to be no hardship at all. After taking in the sky, the sea and everything on board, it was time to retire. Sleep came easily in the gentle surroundings of a comfortable ship.

Most passengers rise early after night crossings. There are important things to do before disembarkation. Everyone becomes purposeful and even harried. Suitcases are lugged through narrow corridors and stacked in the foyer and along the promenade deck. As cabins are vacated, stewards move in to clean them and make up the beds. Passengers line the rails for their first view of a new land or pick out some familiar point of reference. For most, relaxation that set in after departure has vanished even before the voyage is over. Passengers are thinking ahead about the different world ashore.

After rounding the northern tip of the island at Cap Corse, the *Sampiero Corso* followed the coastline, dominated by an unbroken chain of 3000-foot peaks. Before 7 a.m., the ship entered the port of Bastia and tied up at a long berth running parallel to the town, laid out attractively on a narrow flat strip of land. Travellers anxious to disembark crowded the gangway and slowly began filing off the ship.

Bastia is one of those convenient places where nearly everything is within a short walk. Our needs were only two - breakfast and a car hire. At a freshly hosed down waterfront café within sight of the unloading ship, we had the typical fare of croissants and coffee.

For our transportation across the island, we chose another 2 CV whose motor operated with the sound of a sewing machine and seemed to have about as much power. It became nothing short of a challenge to navigate the steep, quaint mountain roads. With the accelerator to the floor most of the time, we bucked and swayed along the north coast stopping at Calvi for lunch and the hill town of Piana for the night.

Around mid-morning on the second day, we drove into Ajaccio, the port city where Napoleon Bonaparte was born in 1769. By that time Corsica had changed its allegiance from Italy to France, otherwise Europe's history might have been quite different. Napoleon's birthplace was a few steps from the Citadel, city hall and the maritime station.

The newish car ferry *Napoléon* had arrived from Marseilles and was berthed just ahead of the *Cyrnos*. The *Napoléon*'s modern lines and white hull presented a marked contrast to the now elderly, black-hulled little *Cyrnos*. In two years, the three remaining classic ships would be replaced by newer car ferry tonnage designed for fast turn arounds and more day crossings. They could make a round trip between the mainland and Corsica in 24 hours rather than sitting all day in port as did the traditional night boats. As a result they would become far more economical to operate and much less interesting in which to travel.

Later that same day, we crossed through the island's centre, left off the car and reboarded the *Sampiero Corso* for the overnight crossing to Nice. The after-dinner sailing at 9 p.m. was lightly patronised and most pleasant. The cabin faced onto the enclosed promenade deck, and we were entertained with glimpses of passing strollers and snatches of audible conversation.

The ship docked early the next morning in the tight little harbour at Villefranche and by 7:30 we were rapping on the door of our parents' room at the Hotel Negresco located on the Promenade des Anglais. Following a three-day family reunion on the French Riviera, we all returned to Paris on the second section of the all Wagons-Lits *Blue Train*, steam-powered as far as Marseilles.

Chapter Four

Student Crossing

SS Rotterdam

HOLLAND AMERICA'S
SS ROTTERDAM
New York-Southampton, September 1966

Up to the summer of 1966, I had a window on the Hudson River at Holland America Line's Pier 40 where I worked in the newly-established sales promotion department. Prior to that posting, I had been at the company's Fifth Avenue passenger office on the phones, then in direct sales. Holland America acted as agents for all Dutch passenger-carrying lines with a total of about 500 ships on which I could book space. The non-HAL lines were referred to as Dutch World Services, and I was the only clerk who seemed interested in handling them as they required much additional study, a good knowledge of geography, constant telexes and often long waits for replies.

The largest demand came for Royal Netherlands Steamship Company's (KNSM) small 12-passenger freighters sailing from Brooklyn to Jamaica, Haiti, Venezuela and Surinam. The Haitian passengers were the most difficult because they tried to bring aboard all sorts of appliances, televisions and stereo equipment under the guise of personal baggage. When the company discovered that I spoke French, I was

Holland America's 38,645-ton *Rotterdam,* later known mainly as one of the World's finest cruise ships, was also one of the last great transatlantic express liners. *Laurence Dunn Collection.*

This 1963 aerial shot shows Holland America's *Rotterdam* docked on the south side of Pier 40, the passenger cargo liner *Westerdam* parallel to the river, and the twin-funnelled *Nieuw Amsterdam* on the north side, with her bow blocking the author's future office view. The large open square pier was designed to handle the new container trade as well as to provide company offices and both indoor and outdoor parking for employees and passengers. *Port Authority of New York & New Jersey.*

assigned to assist at embarkation, and to make sure there was no mistake, because of language miscommunication, about what went into the cabin and what was charged as freight. Many of these passengers were regulars, couriers who flew up to New York and sailed home with the goods to fill orders or to flog in Port au Prince and Cap Haitien. I have never argued more in my life, but thankfully the Haitian sailings were only once a fortnight.

One idea which took off in a small way was to create round-the-world sea tours joining up several Dutch lines. The only missing link was trans-Pacific, so we established an interchange agreement with American President Lines, using their *President Cleveland* and *President Wilson* from California to Japan. From here on, it was all Dutch, first with Royal Interocean Lines' monthly sailings via Hong Kong and Singapore to South Africa, then one of Holland Africa's *'fontein'* trio north to Amsterdam and Holland America from Rotterdam back to New York or directly to the West Coast via Panama aboard the 60-passenger *Dinteldyk* or *Diemerdyk*. I made land arrangements for the intervals between ships and wrote the brochure copy.

Bon voyage cards and gifts of flowers, fruit or wine were a traditional send-off for travellers by sea. *Author's Collection.*

But mostly it was selling Holland America transatlantic voyages and cruises from New York, and in the mid-1960s the fleet consisted of the *Nieuw Amsterdam*, *Rotterdam*, *Statendam*, *Maasdam*, *Ryndam* and *Prinses Margriet.* Then in the summer, we represented the chartered sailings for the student ships *Groote Beer* and *Seven Seas.* By my time, the *Waterman* and *Zuiderkruis* were no longer coming to New York. Eastbound sailings from mid-June into

***Rotterdam* in New York's Upper Bay with a railroad car float heading for Brooklyn and the Manhattan skyline in the background.** *Holland America Line.*

The 38,645-ton *Rotterdam* passes beneath the Verrazano-Narrows Bridge before heading out into the Atlantic, 16th September 1966.
Theodore W. Scull.

July were always wait-listed as were August sailings westbound. Some people just showed up at the pier hoping to get aboard, and when overbookings occurred, we used extra cots and even the hospital wards

In the Fifth Avenue office, passengers paid the published fares, though some might get a guarantee of a category and could later end up with a better cabin. Travel agents fared better in getting a cabin when space was tight. A pre-Christmas visit to the berthing boys' room on Pier 40 reminded us why.

In the days of segregation in America, the company had a policy not to mix whites and blacks in the same cabin. As a clerk, if I had a black person seated at my desk, I had to work the code word "*Zuiderkruis*" into any phone request for a berth assignment. The designation referred to a Dutch government ship that had transported West Indians between islands during the sugar cane cutting and banana picking seasons. One day a black man came in wanting a berth on a sailing to Southampton. During my phone conversation with reservations on the pier, I could not bring myself to say "*Zuiderkruis.*" When the man left, I phoned back, and I was given hell, because now he would have to be offered another cabin, and I would have to write up a new confirmation for his deposit and send it out.

Some of us played a game as prospective passengers made their way to one of our desks. We would guess if he or she was a *Nieuw Amsterdam* first-class passenger, *Maasdam* or *Ryndam* tourist, *Rotterdam* Christmas cruise or just someone who was tired shopping and wanted to sit down and reminisce about a last crossing. It passed the time and we kept score. I was considered a good salesman but I spent too long with the clients, so the office manager used to say, though he talked endlessly with everyone.

When I transferred to the pier, I found it a lively place to work, and my lunch hours were taken on the roof parking lot watching the cargo handling or going aboard one of the passenger ships and sitting in an empty lounge with my brown bag. My favorite venues were the tiny first class lounges aboard the *Maasdam* or *Ryndam* and some 15 years later I got to use one as a passenger during a ten-day crossing on the *Stefan Batory*.

The steamship business was changing, and most people did not see much of a future. The transatlantic schedules got trimmed a bit each year, and that trade was definitely going downhill except in the summer months. The cruising side did not interest me much so I handed in my resignation and decided to accept a place at the University of London's School of Oriental and African Studies and read for a masters' degree.

I had never sailed in a Holland America Line ship as two weeks' holiday was not enough time to cross to Europe and back, so I decided to book the *Rotterdam*. The dates worked and she had the fleet's most comfortable tourist class. I got no discount, being a former non-pensioned employee, but the company did specify 'KIP' or keep alone if possible. I ended up with inside two-berth Cabin 445 to myself all the way aft on Main Deck. It was pure luxury to have a single as previous tourist class crossings aboard the *Hanseatic*, *Kungsholm*, and *Sylvania* had involved two or three cabin mates.

The *List of Passengers* had five pages of advertisements including the announcement for s.s. *Rotterdam*'s 7th annual *Around the World in 80 Days*, sailing from New York on January 24, 1967. Rates from $2800. Another touted the s.s. *Ryndam*'s two 107-day semesters at sea under the aegis of Chapman College in Orange, California. The Library Steward was listed as selling sets of six colour slides of the ships for $1.00 and H.M. Le Fleming's 77-page booklet *Ships of the Holland America Line* was available for $1.75. The ship's Commander was listed as Commodore A. de Jong, while the Chief Steward was C.A. de Jong.

The vast majority of the 850 tourist-class passengers listed were, like me, headed to Britain or Europe for post-graduate studies. Bon voyage parties packed the public rooms and cabins and spilled out into the corridors as

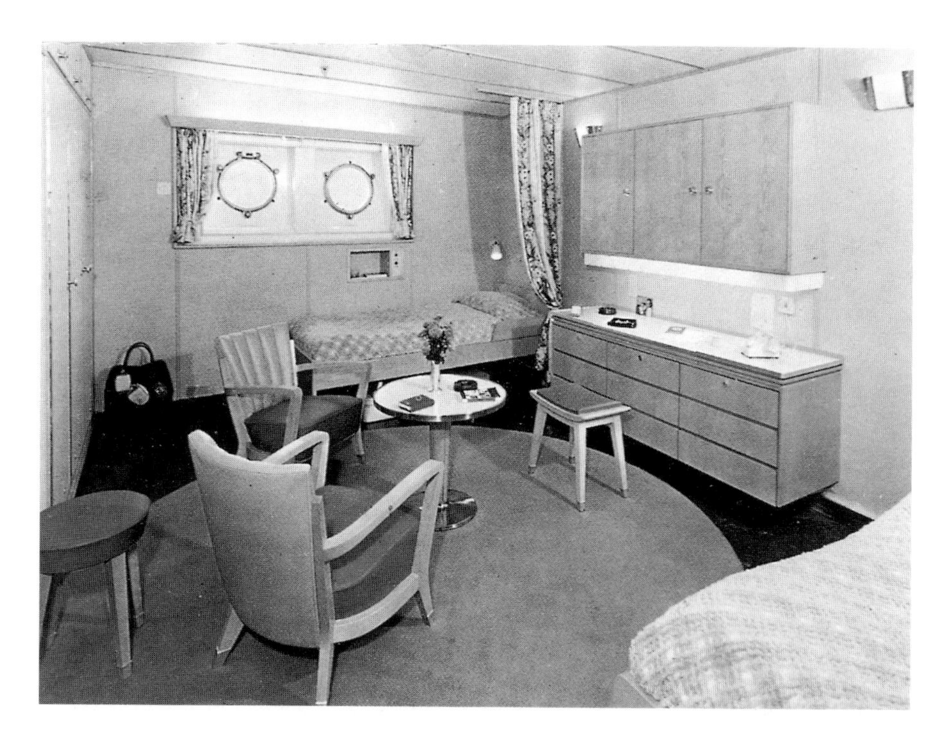

1950s-style furnishings and far-apart twin beds are highlighted features of this roomy, outside first-class double cabin aboard the *Rotterdam*. *Author's Collection.*

The Ocean Bar on the *Rotterdam* was one of the favourite watering holes on the high seas. *Author's Collection.*

hundreds of parents, grandparents, aunts, uncles and siblings bad farewell for a year or longer. My own parents had sailed a few weeks before aboard the *Michelangelo* for Naples, so with my brother at university in Ohio, it was a few friends and two former colleagues who saw me off When it was time to sail, the send-off moved to the top deck of Pier 40 to watch the *Rotterdam* reverse into the river.

The ship crossed paths with the Erie-Lackawanna Railroad's Barclay Street Ferry and Jersey Central's Liberty Street Ferry, the one gone and the other about to go when I returned over a year later. The handsome *Leonardo da Vinci* steamed slowly behind and the *Rotterdam* made her way through Upper New York Bay paralleling the route of the Staten Island Ferry for a few miles then slid beneath the less than two-year-old Verrazano-Narrows Bridge.

In the baggage hold, I had stowed two steamer trunks and six suitcases bearing what I would need to maintain an existence in a furnished bed-sitter located somewhere in London. As nearly everyone else was literally and figuratively in the same boat, we used the week to work

Ted Scull stands alongside the Southern Region's *Ocean Liner Express* - name board reads "Holland American" - preparing to take passengers off the *Rotterdam* up to Waterloo. *Donald Linky.*

Rotterdam **eases away from Southampton's Ocean Terminal to call at Le Havre, then sail overnight to the home port of Rotterdam, on 23rd September, 1966.** *Theodore W. Scull.*

out our anxieties about studying at a foreign university and living in a strange country, something present and future generations will never have a chance to do on the high seas, as less than a day after they leave home they have arrived.

The surroundings were more spacious than I had ever experienced travelling tourist class. We had an entire deck of public rooms, with five lounges, a glass-enclosed promenade, a proper cinema, a near top-of-the-ship Sun Room, an outdoor pool and use of the indoor pool at specified hours. The La Fontaine Restaurant was a grand two-deck-high-space with a dazzling ceramic tile ceiling, and it was almost identical to the first-class Odyssey Restaurant. An ingenious double grand staircase and a system of sliding doors separated the classes, so there was very little running into barriers marked with signs that said "First Class Only."

My table companions were graduates from Dartmouth, Princeton, Rutgers, Smith and a university in Zurich, and we had a jolly time at lunch and dinner and at breakfast, if we made it. Buffet dining elsewhere did not exist then, so we were all together for more than a dozen meals

I find re-reading my journal, that my earliest night was midnight because I had a cold, and the rest ranged from 1:30 a.m. to 5:30 a.m. Evenings were passed with bingo or horse racing in the main lounge, and dancing in the Café de la Paix. There was one night of professional entertainment which *To-Day's Program* announced as "*Special entertainment featuring Glen Haywood - 'Mr. Personality' with a Comedy - Novelty Act, and Sherry Stevens, a beautiful girl with a beautiful voice.*" I later learned that the pair enjoyed performing in tourist far more than first as we made a livelier and larger audience.

There was also quite a lot of bending the elbow, mostly Tom Collins, in the Ocean Bar. It became and still is one of my favourite bars on any ship, and then it was a novelty, at least in most tourist classes, to be able to sit next to large windows overlooking the sea.

Days were spent around the pool, playing table tennis on the promenade deck, and seeing the movies *My Fair Lady*, *A Thousand Clowns*, *Torn Curtain* and *Hotel Paradiso*. During one trapshooting session I got five hits out of ten in the morning, and with the wind up, only three in the afternoon.

On the second evening at sea, I was invited, along with one other student to the Captain's Cocktail Party in the Sun Lounge. It was a stiff affair as Commodore de Jong was not a very good social mixer. The other invited student and I became good friends, and we travelled together the following Easter on Royal Mail's *Amazon* to Lisbon and across the Iberian Peninsula to catch a ship to Majorca. On the Gala Night, we had a candlelight dinner and an excellent Dutch Steak Sauté, and the *Variety Show by our Talented Crew members* on the final night was both excellent and pretty terrible.

Upon arrival in Southampton, my cabin steward called me at 6:00 a.m to come out on deck to see the *Queen Elizabeth* pull out of her berth, quite a sight in the early morning light. Disembarkation took place at 8:15 a.m., and as my baggage weighed in 300 pounds overweight, I had to pay British Railways £1-5s-0d excess charges.

The steam-powered boat train pulled out at 10:04 a.m with ten coaches and three luggage vans, arriving at Waterloo at 12:12. Retrieving baggage was a scramble but there were ample porters, and soon my belongings were deposited at a B&B opposite the South Kensington tube station. Next on the docket was registration at the University of London, tuition free, plus a fee of £25 for the external examination at the end. I found a bed-sitter in West Kensington across from Olympia, and it turned out to be an excellent year of studies and travels.

Chapter Five

Sailing to Iberia

RMS Amazon and *MS Patricia*

ROYAL MAIL'S *RMS AMAZON*
London (Tilbury)-Lisbon March/April, 1967

By the spring of 1967, I had been residing in London for six months reading for a master's degree at the School of Oriental and African Studies and enduring a cold, damp winter in a rented bed-sitter without central heating. I had to save shillings for the electric fire, a not so easy task since they were in great demand, six pences for the hot water and coppers for the shared shower. Now with the Easter Holidays in the offing, I looked forward, with a classmate whom I had met coming over on the *Rotterdam*, to heading south for a fortnight in sunny Spain and Portugal.

On our limited budget, we had the choice of train or ship. The rail route to Portugal was an uninviting obstacle course involving the continental boat train from Victoria to Dover Marine or Folkestone Harbour, a British or French railway ferry for Calais Maritime or Boulogne, connecting boat train to Gare du Nord, Metro across Paris, Sud Express night train from Gare d'Austerlitz to the Spanish border, and finally the broad-gauge overnight Lusitania Express for Lisbon. Not taking to this ordeal, especially travelling second class, we investigated the more direct sea route to Vigo in northwest Spain, or to Lisbon. The fare would include a berth and three meals a day for the two- or three-day voyage.

The February, 1967 *ABC Shipping Guide* showed six passenger lines with 13 ships flying the flags of five countries trading between Britain and the Iberian Peninsula. The minimum fares ranged from £11 dormitory-class to £36

The *Amazon* on trials. Note the unusual gap between the bridge structure and the passenger block.
Laurence Dunn Collection.

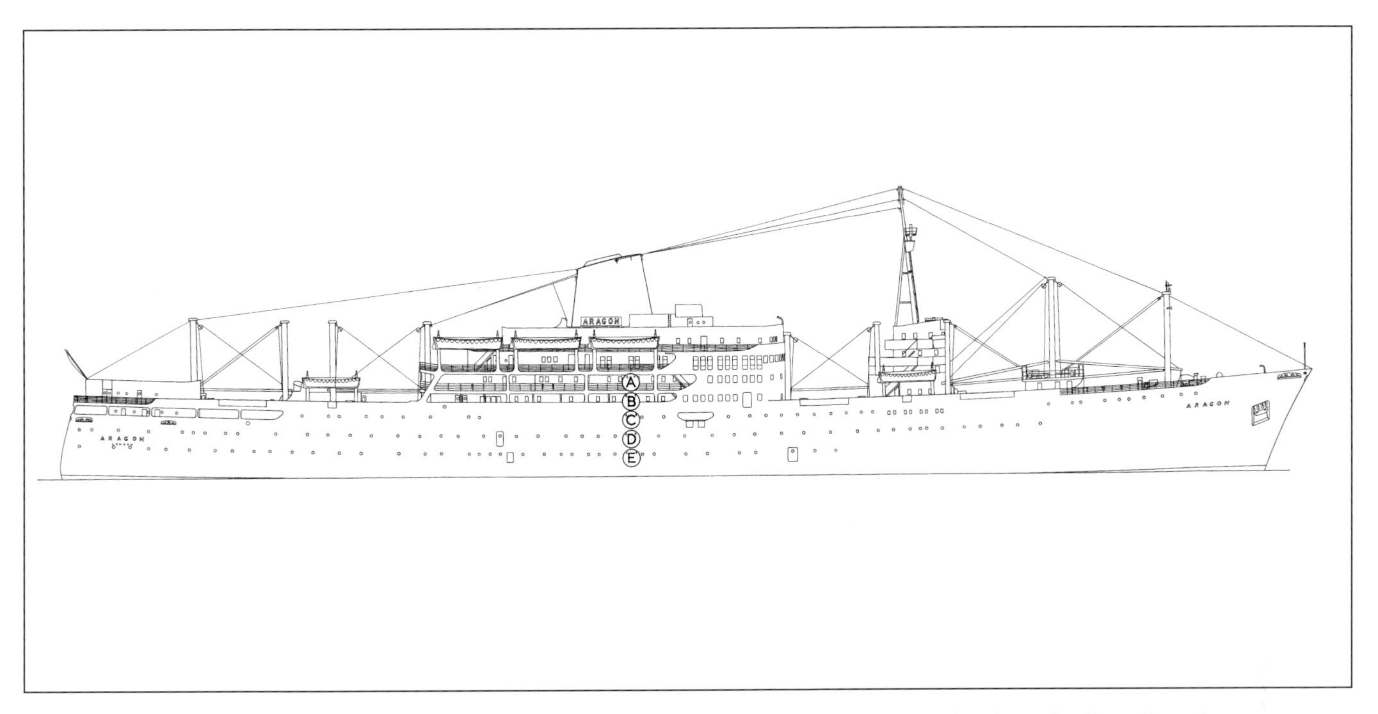

A profile scale drawing of one of the *Amazon's* sister ships, the *Aragon*, emphasises the fact that they were as much cargo-carriers as passenger liners. *Author's Collection.*

in a one-class passenger-cargo ship. We began the process of elimination by making the rounds of the shipping companies, nearly all having stylish ground-floor West End booking offices.

Blue Star Line operated four handsome 10,700-ton cargo liners of the *Argentina Star* class with berths for about 50 passengers between London and the east coast of South America via Lisbon. But the first-class configuration commanded a high fare.

The Argentine State Line's 12,650-ton *Libertad* carried 96 first-class passengers on an infrequent six-week rotation, so it was not surprising when the schedule did not mesh with ours. I eliminated the French Line's large multi-class liners *Antilles* and *Flandre* sailing from Southampton to Vigo and on to the West Indies, having made a transatlantic voyage in the latter and not relishing the idea of sailing third class in the former. The Spanish Line's elderly pair, *Begoña* and *Montserrat*, offered the cheapest fare, at £11 from Southampton to Vigo, but an eight-berth cabin in a rebuilt Victory ship seemed a mite basic.

Siosa Line had recently bought the even more elderly Italian liner *Vulcania* of 1928, and as *Caribia* placed her on a route from Southampton to Vigo and Lisbon and then on to Caribbean ports. Much of her famously luxurious first class remained but she offered dormitory berths for £14.

Recalling inspection visits in New York, her almost steerage-style accommodations with memories of metal plates on the decks and steam pipes running along the overhead passages militated against this one.

The last alternative was one of Royal Mail Lines' A-Class liners sailing from Tilbury Docks via Boulogne to Vigo and Lisbon, a three-night voyage for £20 in third class, the ships continuing to South America. The booking clerk said that the ships generally picked up most lower-class, South America-bound passengers in Spain, Portugal and the Canary Islands, so we would likely have the outside four-berth to ourselves. The date and price were right, so we chose the *RMS Amazon* sailing on 31st March. With rail and steamer tickets in hand, we boarded the boat train at Liverpool Street Station for Tilbury Riverside.

The *Amazon* was the first of three almost identical 20,000-gross-ton, 17.5-knot sisters completed at Harland and Wolff, Belfast between 1959 and 1960 to replace four pre-War *Highland*-class ships. The trio, including the *Aragon* and *Arlanza*, maintained a service at intervals of 21 days between Britain and the east coast of South America.

The twin-screw, turbo-charged diesel ships had three classes of accommodations for about 470 passengers, but most of the money came from freight carried in the five insulated and general-cargo holds, numbers one and two located forward of the bridge, four and five aft of the main superstructure and number three located between the bridge and navigating officers' accommodation and the passenger superstructure. This unusual design was a carry-over from the *Highland*-class ships, and the A-class were certainly the last passenger-cargo ships built to this anachronistic arrangement.

By the time the boat train, arrived at Tilbury Riverside, the *Amazon* had shifted from the cargo-loading inner docks to the passenger landing stage. While her design was old-fashioned, she presented a handsome, streamlined profile, had an all-white hull and superstructure and buff Royal Mail Lines funnel. Before

The author stands near the bow next to the *Amazon's* bell during a passage between London Tilbury, Vigo, and Lisbon on 31st March, 1967. *Donald Linky.*

departure, we explored the first and cabin classes, proportioned like a cozy English country hotel, each with about 100 berths depending on the interchange allocation. The lounge furniture was covered in colourful floral chintz and the walls panelled in a variety of exotic woods, typical of British ships of the day, but also at the very end of the era for this type of décor.

The up and down layout was complex with little chance to walk any distance either fore or aft. The first-class all-facility cabins and their public rooms and deck space occupied the midships or forward portions of six decks, while cabin class was stacked midships and aft on four decks.

Our plain third-class lounge, smoking room and dining room were arranged in a single line on the port side midships and aft. The 273 cabin berths were down on D and E decks, and ours, berths 437 and 438, had two uppers and two lowers, pipe-rack-style, and a wash basin next to a porthole that opened. Baths, showers and separate ladies' and gentlemen's toilets and washplaces were located in a central line.

Each class had its own outdoor swimming pool and promenade, and the tourist-class pool was nearly at the stern next to the isolation hospital on the Sports Deck, while open deck space was aft on B Deck and the covered promenade on the deck below. Besides ladies' and gentlemen's hospital wards, there were separate Spanish and Portuguese dispensaries in addition to the consulting room.

The ship was booked well below capacity. Many passengers were British retirees headed for Lisbon, dividing their time between Britain and the Algarve, plus a number of students getting there on the cheap.

In the early afternoon, we swung away from the landing stage as New Zealand Shipping's 17,850-ton *Ruahine* was arriving on a five-week voyage from Auckland and Wellington with passengers and New Zealand lamb and butter. As she took our place at the landing stage, the *Amazon* moved down the Thames on a parallel course with the Atlantic Steam Navigation Company's 35-passenger *Cerdic Ferry*. In the river we met the outbound P&O *Bendigo* and inbound Shaw Savill's *Ionic* and then overtook one of the Prince Line's pretty cargo-passenger ships en route to the Mediterranean.

The Thames emptied its wide mouth into the North Sea and the *Amazon* went hard to starboard to take aim on the Strait of Dover. From our vantage point at the bow, we watched our ship dodge the cross traffic of fast passenger and passenger-vehicle ferries shuttling between England and France. With no passengers to embark, the *Amazon* bypassed Boulogne altogether and headed into the English Channel.

Darkness fell, and by early morning we were rounding the island of Ushant off the western tip of Brittany in a heavy fog. We could no longer stand at the bow because the forward watch was on duty, but from the same deck just ahead of the bridge, we could hear a variety of booming signals all around us. After listening awhile and with a watch and a piece of paper handy, it was possible to predict the next round of repeating sounds. It was cold, damp and eerie, especially as we could see nothing but our own ship and not even the full length of that.

My first trip through the Bay of Biscay was a bit of a disappointment. There was no storm, only a ground swell that sent the *Amazon* gently pitching for about 24 hours. We spent the day reading and playing Scrabble with a young American couple who had finished their university degrees at Cambridge and were bound for Buenos Aires to make a long South American tour before returning to the States to begin work. They were good table companions, and we remarked that Royal Mail Line third-class food was far better than the university cafeteria fare we were used to, and being a British ship at sea, the beer was good and cheap.

The ship's band played in first and cabin but there was no planned entertainment in tourist. An elderly British passenger took to our piano whenever asked, and that is the gentle way that I spent my twenty-something birthday in the Bay of Biscay.

Royal Mail's *Amazon* is docked at Vigo, northwest Spain, en route from London Tilbury to Buenos Aires, 2nd April, 1967.
Theodore W. Scull.

The *Amazon*'s call at Vigo lasted most of the day. Vehicles were unloaded, and cargo and other vehicles crane-loaded. Vigo's huge maritime station had kiosks for many shipping lines, as the port was on the sea lanes to the West Indies, South America, South Africa, the Mediterranean, Suez, India, Southeast Asia, the Far East, Australia and New Zealand. Nearly a hundred porters dressed in black were in attendance but only a fraction got any work.

We entered the River Tagus on the third morning, and through the open port I saw the former Zim Israel passenger liner *Israel*, now the Portuguese *Angra do Heroismo* leaving port for the Azores. I hurried up on deck to find the docks lined with ships - the nearly brand-new *Funchal* purpose-built for the Azores, the colonial liners *Imperio* and *Mocambique* embarking Portuguese peasant farmers for resettlement in Angola and Mozambique, the Greek Line's transatlantic *Queen Anna Maria* en route to New York, and Moore-McCormack's *Brasil* and Norwegian America's *Oslofjord* on cruises. It was a thrilling catch for a single day.

Additional liners showed up on successive mornings, repeatedly drawing us down to the docks during our four-day stay. We then crossed the Iberian Peninsula by train, stopping in Madrid, and embarked at Granada for the overnight run to Palma de Majorca aboard the Compañía Trasmediterránea's classic 4,944-ton passenger vessel *Ciudad de Granada*, built in 1960, returning a week later via the brand-new ferry *Juan March* to Barcelona, a roll-on ship of nearly 10,000-tons. The three Spanish ports offered a survey of one of the most varied, and certainly the oldest, fleet in the Mediterranean. Two veteran vessels seen were the 1911-built *Rey Jaime I* and the 1914-built *Mallorca*, but with several new car ferry series in the process of being introduced, the numerous pre-World War II units would soon be withdrawn.

The Portugese liner *Mocambique*, belonging to the Cia. Nacional de Navegação, is loading migrants (as part of a resettlement scheme for peasant farmers) and colonial staff, mail and cargo at Lisbon for a voyage out to Angola, South Africa and Mozambique, 5th April, 1967.
Theodore W. Scull.

SWEDISH LLOYD'S *MS PATRICIA*
Bilbao-Southampton, April 1967

Following a night in Barcelona, my travelling companion went off to Italy and I boarded a TER train to Bilbao and the next day had some difficulty in tracking down the Swedish Lloyd office which had recently moved to an unmarked location one level up from the street. The agents could not book me a cabin as the berthing list was down at the port at Santurce, a ten-mile train ride away.

The brand-new *Patricia* looked very smart indeed tied up amongst the debris of new dock construction and ancient Spanish shipping. Docked nearby was the Spanish Line's handsome *Covadonga* of 1953 operating a passenger and cargo service on a triangular route between Spain, the West Indies, Mexico and New York and Nederland Line's *Bali*, a cargo-passenger ship commissioned in 1947 and presently on a Far Eastern run.

The minimum rate of £8 for the 36-hour passage to Southampton meant another four-berth cabin, and on this ship, below the vehicle deck. For an extravagant £14, I booked a berth in a double, that is only the two lower berths would be sold, returned to Bilbao by train and embarked later in the afternoon.

A brochure dated November, 1969 for Swedish Lloyd's car ferry liners *Patricia*, *Hispania* and *Saga*, running between Southampton and Bilbao; and Tilbury and Gothenburg. *Author's Collection.*

Completed at Gothenburg earlier in the year, the 7,900-ton *Patricia* represented a new breed of short-sea ferry liner, where vehicles could be driven directly aboard and passengers travelled in a single class, albeit to an ingenious design that subtly separated the economic classes. On the North Sea, Swedish Lloyd and the Svea Line operated two near-sisters, *Saga* and *Svea* between Tilbury and Gothenburg while Ellerman's Wilson operated the *Spero* from Hull.

The Saloon Deck had two sets of linear public rooms, with a centre divider running fore an aft. On the port side,

Swedish Lloyd's brand-new passenger and vehicle ferry *Patricia* at Bilbao, awaiting embarkation for Southampton on 17th April, 1967. *Theodore W. Scull.*

those who would choose to eat in the forward Cafeteria would naturally gravitate to the lounge, bar and gallery leading to that facility, while on the starboard side, a second set of more expensively furnished bars and lounges led straight into the sit-down restaurant.

In addition, the ship had another lounge aft on the deck below, a small children's playroom, chapel, shop, teenage room right up at the bow below the car deck, outdoor swimming pool and my first experience of a casino at sea. Its sophisticated atmosphere was certainly alluring to a non-gambler, and I managed to have an enjoyable evening at the roulette table without recording a loss.

I ended up with sole occupancy of Cabin 308, below the car deck, and the Gents and showers were located just a few steps away. On my bed was a notice that said, 'Kindly remember, however, that this is a brand-new ship, and it is possible that certain details in your cabin, or in the public rooms, might require some adjustments, or improvements.' Below the notice was a large space for comments and suggestions, but none were needed. The car deck was nearly full, and the cabins, nearly all four berth rooms with and without en suite facilities, about half occupied on this 17th April sailing.

The *Patricia* sailed from Bilbao at 6:30 p.m. and spent the next entire day in the Bay of Biscay in weather pleasant enough to read outside on the Boat Deck verandah and play some ping pong without having to compensate for a heaving deck. The day and evening were relaxed and uneventful, and the only confusion involved the British and Scandinavian crew becoming used to Spanish currency conversion in the bars, cafeteria, shops and casino.

On the second morning, we sailed up to Southampton on a clear morning following *Viking I* on which I had made a return maiden voyage in 1964. I was able to photograph Shaw Savill's *Northern Star* and have partial and more distant views of the *Queen Elizabeth*, a Union-Castle cargo ship, and P&O-Orient Line's *Oronsay*, the five exhibiting a colourful spectrum of orange, green, black, lavender and white hulls.

We tied up at the new Princess Alexandra berth in the old railway docks, and a shilling coach transfer had me at Southampton Central for the 0822 for Waterloo. I was back in my West Kensington flat by 10:30 to face a three-week heap of mail and a dissertation due by June.

Chapter Six

RMS Queen Elizabeth

The voyage home & The end of an era

CUNARD'S RMS QUEEN ELIZABETH
Southampton-New York October, 1967

Wednesday, 11th October, 1967

I had wound up my affairs and was leaving England following 13 months at the University of London reading for and earning a master's degree. It had been my best academic year ever.

At 3:30 p.m. I rushed out into the High Street to look for a taxi and found one in five minutes, stacking eight suitcases and one trunk inside with no trouble at all. Arriving Waterloo Station, I found the platform jammed with milling First and Cabin passengers. The tourist-class boat train had already left separately at 4 p.m. My baggage exceeded the 100-pound limit by 340 pounds and excess charges came to £1-10s-0d. The crowd stood about nervously, a few with bewildered dogs on leashes, amidst heaps of suitcases, steamer trunks, bulging cardboard containers and cat boxes, but all was order again several minutes after the train pulled in.

We departed promptly at 4:37, raced non-stop down to the spur threading through Southampton Docks and arrived at the Ocean Terminal at 6:30 p.m. The cavernous embarkation lounge was the most evocative space of any maritime station I had ever seen. Although completed about five years after the War, the lighted and shiny metal lettering,

The *Queen Elizabeth* being assisted to her Southampton berth by a fleet of tugs and tug tenders including the *Gatcombe* seen beneath the bridge wing. *Author's Collection.*

The massive twin funnels of the *Queen Elizabeth* dominate this scene during an Atlantic crossing in 1947.
Arthur J. Ferguson.

polished wood panelling, and leather furnishings reflected an Art Deco-moderne-style. A towering world globe formed the centrepiece with the dominant colour red splashed across the continents indicating the expanse of the British Empire. The Ocean Terminal aptly matched the scale of the ship I was about to board, the mighty 83,673-ton *Queen Elizabeth,* the largest passenger liner in the World.

My cabin, D291, was minimum rate Cabin Class on the lowest deck at a fare of $281 plus $2.30 in port tax. It was small but adequate, with an upper and lower berth and toilet. My cabin mate, Fred, an old man from Hull, Yorkshire, spent about half his time in Britain and the other half in the U.S. I opened a GPO telegram from my West Kensington landlady - BON VOYAGE DEAR BOY DONT FORGET PASSENGER LIST EVERY GOOD WISH - CONSTANCE WARD. My friends, two Davids, Frank and Edi were all awaiting me in the Lido Bar which, contrary to Cunard's London office advice was closed, as were all the other bars. I was upset at the thought of not being able to entertain my friends who had come all this way from London. The Cabin Class public rooms were empty, and the dining room was full. I tried to get them in for dinner, but it was a heavy sailing and this was not possible. After some doing, I managed to get a hold of the wine steward and he promptly brought two bottles of Moet to the bar, which the bar steward then said was illegal. So we went below to my tiny cabin, and I produced sandwiches, three each. I then bought two more bottles at $5 each and corks popped until 8:45.

We toured the ship, which was really hideous in style, except for a room here and there, mostly in first class. This ship was certainly not the *Queen Mary,* which had scale and charm while the *Queen Elizabeth*'s post-War decor was heavy and rather dreary, with some strikingly misguided attempts at modernising, such as the plastic palm leaves clinging to the columns in the Caribbean Room. We tramped all over the ship, from the kennels down to my cabin on D-Deck, then at 9:15 they left via the gangway to catch the last direct train up to London. It was a sad parting after a wonderful year together.

I gazed out through the rain for a while, and I could see the *Queen Mary* off in the distance with illuminated funnels and just ahead, the *S. A. Oranje.* I went to bed at 10:00 but not to sleep as it was quite noisy around me and I was still keyed up.

Thursday, 12th October

I awoke to the vibration of the props at 6:45 a.m., got up and dressed quickly for a look around. In the half darkness, I found the *Queen Mary* still lit up but not *S. A. Oranje.* The *Queen Mary* had been sold to the City of Long Beach and would leave Southampton for the last time on 31st October. We sailed down Southampton Water past Bergen Line's *Venus,* a United States Lines freighter and an Elders & Fyffes banana boat. In the Solent, we then met Shaw Savill's *Northern Star,* looking rather small, in-bound from New Zealand and Australia. She was listing under the weight of passengers lining the decks to view the *Q.E.* With a full tide, we sailed out via the Needles, always an unexpected treat.

Breakfast was at 9:00, but with no table reservation in the cabin, I faced a long queue. We arrived Cherbourg at noon in a light drizzle, and the boat train from Paris came alongside at 12:15. We embarked an unknown number of passengers and 25 cars. At lunch, I met my table companions for the next five days: a Polish-American gentleman, dressed in a dark three-piece suit and club tie, very severe-looking and speaking broken English; a 21 year-old fellow from Manchester emigrating to Atlanta, Georgia to work for Lockheed; a thoroughly California couple from Pasadena who 'always fly' everywhere; and a huge English woman on her way to visit her daughter in Seattle, travelling on from New York by train. She boasted that she gained seven stone (98 pounds) in the last year and loved it. It was not exactly a sterling group.

We departed from Cherbourg at 3:30 p.m. followed by drinks in the Caribbean Room with my Yorkshire cabin mate. Dinner at 8:00, and the roast beef and Yorkshire Pudding were excellent. To start things off, I bought a bottle of red wine.

"Some further insights into the table mates. The Polish-American is a professional concert singer and rather full of himself. He gets a free passage in return for an evening's work in each class. The fat lady is mysterious, as she first says she lives in London S.W., then E.C. (Tower Hill). I later saw that her address was Aldgate East. After dinner, I went to the First Class cinema and enjoyed *Triple Cross* with Yul Brynner and Romy Schneider. Out on the Promenade Deck about 11:45, I met an American and Cunard traveller, and we talked about ships for an hour."

Friday, 13th October

I awoke to the vibrations and noise of reversing screws and anchor being lowered. Up on deck, the sun was out and we were moored in Cobh harbor. The old *Innisfallen* passed by and I got a photograph. A tender came alongside with passengers both embarking and disembarking, and we sailed promptly at 9:00. The weather began deteriorating shortly after noon, about the same time we passed close to the southwestern tip of Ireland and the small port of Baltimore, Bantry Bay, where soon giant supertankers of 200,000 tons would discharge their oil. The headlines in the *Ocean Times* that morning were, "B.E.A. Comet 4B Crashes into the Mediterranean - No Survivors Amongst 59 Passengers and Seven Crew." It happened be Friday, the 13th.

I hoped to swim but the pool was so rough I decided against it. Three people were in the pool but they had to hold tightly onto the end rail as the water crashed against the side. I met a gentleman in the Midships Bar who had come over on the *Queen Mary* on her last voyage. Others must have done the same thing which explains, in part, why there were 450 First Class in October and 580 in Cabin. Three table companions did not show at dinner,

A 10-page booklet aimed at impressing passengers with size, capacity, facilities, amenities and food consumption. The listed woods used aboard the *Queen Elizabeth* run from 'A' to 'Z', including Avodire, bubinga, makore, patapsko pomla, petula and zebrano. *Author's Collection.*

A card of the *Queen Elizabeth* and ABSTRACT OF THE LOG given to passengers at the end of a voyage from New York to Southampton via Cherbourg 21st-26th September, 1949. The average speed was recorded at 27.35 knots. *Author's Collection.*

ABSTRACT OF THE LOG OF THE
CUNARD WHITE STAR
R.M.S. "QUEEN ELIZABETH"
Commodore C. M. Ford, C.B.E., R.D., R.N.R.
NEW YORK via CHERBOURG TO SOUTHAMPTON

Date (1949)	Dist.	Latitude	Longitude	Weather, etc.
		N.	W.	
Wed. Sep. 21				At 05.02 E.D.S.T., Left Pier 90, New York.
,, ,, 21				At 07.15 E.D.S.T., Departure A.C.L.V
,, ,, 21	123	40.15	71.09	Gentle breeze, slight sea
Thurs. ,, 22	653	41.22	56.53	Moderate breeze, slight sea
Fri. ,, 23	661	44.38	42.53	Fresh breeze, moderate sea and swell
Sat. ,, 24	643	48.15	28.12	Moderate gale, rough sea, heavy swell
Sun. ,, 25	633	49.46	12.16	Moderate breeze, slight sea, cloudy
Mon. ,, 26	415	to Cherbourg	Breakwater	At 06.36 F.S.T. Arrival Cherbourg Breakwater
Mon. ,, 26		64 miles to	Nab Tower	Departure Cherbourg, at 09.06 F.S.T.
				At 11.54 B.S.T. Nab Tower abeam
Total	3,128	miles		

PASSAGE, New York to Cherbourg - 4 days, 18 hours, 21 minutes
AVERAGE SPEED - 27.35 knots

and there was no cabaret as the singer was seasick. The ship was creaking and groaning, so she might not have been heard anyway. I was asked to dance by a girl from Youngstown, Ohio, but it was difficult because of the motion and not having taken a step since the *Rotterdam* on the way over. The ship was pitching and rolling heavily when I went to bed at 11:00p.m.

Saturday, 14th October

I could not sleep in so got up at 7:15, and the sea was quite rough now. The forward windows in the Observation Bar were boarded up and it was no longer possible to see ahead. I climbed to the deck forward of the aft funnel and watched the sea for some time. The wind was whistling through the wires and at times the ship was heaving violently. First one sees the sea, then one doesn't and I got lashed with spray all the way up there.

I took a Dramamine just in case and felt fine until table mate Barry and I got laughing about the Polish singer, then I did feel slightly ill. Mrs. California came down alone and said she was tired of all the pitching and wished she had flown home. They had thought of a world cruise on the *President Roosevelt* but this experience had finished off that idea. I attempted, without much success, to convince her that crossing the North Atlantic in October was not a fair comparison to sailing around the World in mostly tropical waters.

As I was about to face my parents in New York, I had a haircut for 7s plus 2s tip. At 11:00, I took an hour's walk about the ship up to the Sun Deck. The moon was out, the sea fairly calm, nobody was about. Black smoke was pouring out of the forward stack and was swept over the lifeboats by the forward motion of the ship. The twin funnels were huge and impressive, especially at night. It was a most peaceful experience and unlike any other, to be aboard a ship charging through the night. I was glad that I chose the *Queen Elizabeth.*

Sunday, 15th October

The *Ocean Times* headline read "Severe Marine Losses in Viet-Cong Raid." After lunch we saw a Pathe News film entitled *Launching of Queen Elizabeth II*, presented as an upbeat new era for Cunard, a company that could use some good news following the sell-off of much of its fleet. The main feature was *The Bobo* with Peter Sellers and Britt Ekland. Dinner was uproarious with wine and laughs. "What an unusual assortment of people at one table and still able to get along. After dinner, the Polish singer sang Gypsy songs. He had a good voice and was a real exhibitionist, moving about the floor and shaking his body. I ventured up to First Class to seek out the Spanish girl with whom I had done the puzzle. I had guessed that

The *Queen Mary*, preparing to sail to Long Beach California, gets up steam just ahead of P&O-Orient Line's *Oriana*, (a name for Queen Elizabeth I), October, 1967. *Frank Jackson.*

she was 21, and found that Christina was only 16 and was of German origin from Caracas. Her father and I were the only men not in black tie. Commodore Marr made some amusing remarks after the barely bearable fancy-hat contest. He is entirely at ease in front of a huge room of passengers. I understand he is very disappointed at being prematurely retired at the withdrawal of the *Q.E.* next year. Warwick takes command of the new ship and is currently ashore advising on the fitting out of the new *Q.E.*"

Monday, 16th October

In the morning, I played Ping-Pong and took a swim in the indoor pool. As the ship kept altering course, the water piled up at one side for a minute or so, changing the level a couple of feet. It felt like swimming up and down hill. I took one last tour of the ship and went to bed at 1:30.

Tuesday, 17th October

It was a beautiful, clear, warm day, and by 2:30, Long Island was in view. As we neared the Verrazano-Narrows Bridge, it appeared as if the forward mast would hit the span's underside. When we actually made it, by inches it seemed, the passengers on deck broke out in spontaneous applause and cheers. We passed the *Finnmaid*, *Concordia Lago* and the Spanish Line's *Covadonga* in Upper New York Bay. I organized my tips with £1-10s-0d to the waiter, £2-0s-0d to the cabin steward and 7s. 0d in loose change to the deck steward. The ship docked at 5:15 p.m. instead of the scheduled 8:00 a.m. The storm after Cobh made us miss the tide by a few hours, so we had to amble in and waste time. I saw Pop down at street level and finally attracted his attention. This was really a superb trip and just long enough. The ship was grand though the Cabin Class public rooms were quite unattractive. First Class was much better with high ceilings, and Tourist had poor facilities except for the Observation Bar (originally First Class). The food was very good and plentiful if not exciting, and the service efficient with the bare minimum of chatter from the waiter and cabin steward.

I was off the ship at 5:45 and then endured a long wait for baggage with 1,702 other passengers. The shed was fairly chaotic but I was really in no hurry and it would have been no good if I was anyway. All my suitcases arrived within one hour but there was no trunk to be seen. The 72 cars would be off-loaded the next morning, so Barry would spend the night on board. The Cabin baggage had gotten mixed up with the Tourist baggage so I waited until 8:30 for the trunk to come. The customs officer made a thorough examination of every (nine) piece, then I was off the pier by 9:00. Mother and Father were there, and we drove home in a rented station wagon, arriving at 10:45. After a late supper, I went to bed very tired indeed, but it had been an exhilarating day and a wonderful homecoming.

The *Queen Elizabeth* is taking on fuel at Pier 90, New York, while the combination passenger-cargo ship *Parthia* is working a bulk commodity at Pier 92. *Port Authority of New York and New Jersey.*

The former *Queen Elizabeth* lies a burnt-out wreck after a fire, believed to be arson, broke out on 9th January, 1972 in Hong Kong harbour. The great liner was due to re-enter service as the *Seawise University*, a round-the-World school ship owned by the shipping magnate C. Y. Tung. *Author's Collection.*

Chapter Seven

French Line Tradition Lives

SS France

CGT'S *SS FRANCE*
Southampton-New York June/July, 1968

I cut classes to be in New York when the *S.S. France* arrived on her maiden voyage in February, 1962. A friend from university and I came into Grand Central on the New Haven Railroad from Hartford, then took the Lexington Avenue IRT subway down to the Battery arriving in time to watch the fireboats escort the French Line's new 1035-foot liner past the Statue of Liberty. The *France* was a grand sight, a towering, sleek greyhound with a *Normandie* bow line and winged funnels, and much better looking than shown as drawings in *Popular Science* magazine.

As the *France* received and responded to greetings from other ships in the harbour, we plunged back into the subway and once uptown, literally ran from Broadway to the river just as the ship was angling into the slip between piers. There were hundreds of people gathered at street level, lots of French overheard and free coffee and croissants being handed out in celebration.

Back at university late that afternoon, I found a note from the dean under my dormitory door. An enthusiastic explanation did not pass muster, and he restricted me to campus for a week for missing classes without permission.

In the period from 1962 to 1967 I made four transatlantic crossings, and in June, 1968 I was in London on the last leg of an around-World sea trip. I was so full of ships that I applied for a job with P&O but in an interview at Beaufort House, I was told that there was a moratorium on hiring for the passenger department. When nothing more looked like panning out, I went to the French Line office in Cockspur Street and booked a minimum passage aboard the *France* to New York for $256.10 using my open BOAC ticket as payment.

As I was travelling on an interchange round-the-World ticket, and the last leg was originally scheduled to be by air to Philadelphia, I had to buy a $10 air ticket from BOAC to complete the 90-mile journey from New York, my port of entry by sea.

My best friend in England drove me down to Southampton Docks in a Mini van, and we drew up to the Ocean Terminal just as the *France* was arriving from Le Havre.

She was a tremendously impressive sight and made the Cunarder *Caronia*, docked nearby and just recently sold, look positively dowdy and the pretty little Elders & Fyffes' *Golfito* a ship in miniature.

We departed at 11 p.m., with five tugs assisting. I stood in the bright light of the letter "E" and waved to my friend way below on the dock apron. I felt a bit sad leaving England, and worried about what to do with my life when I reached New York.

I discovered that first class, even in port, was not easy to penetrate, and I was politely turned out of the beautiful Art Deco aft smoking room, the best looking public space on the ship. During the crossing, the way into first class was through the Galeries Lafayette shop and up the stairs to Veranda Deck. I could then make it to the open decks without attracting attention, and I enjoyed climbing to within earshot of the squash court. While I was not allowed to play, I liked hearing the slapping of the hard black rubber ball against the walls.

My cabin mate did not show, though his bags did, so I ended up having B-508, most assuredly deserving the designation of propeller suite, to myself. The bulkhead sloped inward and the porthole was set back into the hull. It leaked when the sea kicked up, but the cabin steward made a kind of barrage with towels, changed periodically when they became too sodden to hold back the sea.

In spite of the churning props, I slept so well that first night I had no idea what day it was when I finally woke. The steward must have come in during the wee hours because the deadlight was firmly in place over the glass.

Happily, in true French Line style, I landed a great table with four American girls fresh from studies in France, a psychology teacher from Rhode Island and a young Italian who spoke French and practically no English. The menu was tops, certainly better than anything I had tasted at sea since the French liner *Laos* back at the beginning of February, and the festive atmosphere was enhanced by complimentary red and white table wines that were replenished without asking. The wines were 'gutsy' according to one brochure, as they were fortified with Algerian varieties. The voyage looked promising, apart from having to think about facing my Father on the pier in New York.

The *France* was a thoroughly modern ship with rather spare décor in tourist class and not a great choice of public rooms. In fact, there were just two lounges, one huge

The last great French transatlantic liner, the *France*, with her characteristic winged funnels.
Laurence Dunn Collection.

Billet de Passage for a guarantee of a Tourist Class berth at minimum rate for a westbound sailing Southampton-New York on 31st August, 1973. The author was assigned B206 Upper Berth B all the way forward on Bordeaux Deck, Value $381.25.
Author's Collection.

room featuring the longest bar afloat at 70 feet and the more attractive Left Bank Café, also with a bar and dance floor. The tourist-class promenade was a delight, with its warm and airy atmosphere contrasting with a blustery gray day beyond the glass. It became a daily ritual to take a stroll and strike up a conversation with a familiar face. Promising exchanges would often result in being invited to sit down at the foot of the deck chair, so a lot of time passed socialising along this grand promenade.

French Line ambiance was firmly in place. The ship was extremely well run and efficient compared to the *Windsor Castle* which I had left 10 days before. The *France* was a true luxury liner, even at the minimum rate, with a crew who cared. On Union-Castle, if you and a steward arrived at a door from opposite sides at the same time, he would walk through first, but not on the *France*.

First class had only 200 passengers while tourist had 900, a much higher proportion of berths booked, and the critical mass made all the staged events a good deal of fun. Even the Ping-Pong tournament, which I did not get very far into, was done with the style that I remembered from the *Liberté*. Tourist class had two bands, and I got to dance again on a lighted coloured glass dance floor, this time without sliding off the edge.

The tourist class pool was aft beneath a dome, a good compromise for the North Atlantic, and I carried on with a before breakfast swim as had been my habit from Durban to Southampton aboard the *Windsor Castle*. The pool was large, good for laps, and had deep recesses to absorb the waves that built up on rough days.

We had a whole gale one day with the sea running in two different directions. Many passengers were sick, and very few came to breakfast. There were lots of stains on the carpets and a heavy smell of disinfectants. Some people were slumped in deck chairs looking as if they wanted to die. This was not the time to stop for a chat.

When there wasn't much going on I took to my bunk, and as I worked through my thoughts, I decided on teaching as a profession. Having no experience other than at a missionary school some years back in Tanganyika, the job would have to be in an independent school, so I collected my reasons for doing so, knowing my Father's first question would be, "Good God, why?" He had been in the family coffee and tea business all his life and would not understand but Mother would. It was almost as if - that's settled, now I can go on enjoying the voyage. Interestingly, the idea of teaching constantly occupied my thoughts.

My happiest place on the ship was high up by the funnels late at night when the illuminated sign *FRANCE* was turned off. There was no one out there to see it anyway. I then remembered what the appearance of the illuminated *ILE DE FRANCE* must have meant to the *Andrea Doria's* passengers as they were evacuating the ship in the dark after colliding with the *Stockholm* off Nantucket in July 1955.

Smoke poured out of the winged funnels like a jet stream giving a sense of great speed and incredible power.

The *France* departing from New York in August, 1973. *Vincent Messina.*

The aft funnel of the *France* dominates this onboard scene photographed in 1973. *Theodore W. Scull.*

Sometimes I stood still looking up at the funnel and then I would walk as fast as I could against the wind and then let it carry me aft. If I did not hold my jacket closed, the force would almost tear one's clothes off. The radar could be heard whirling at different speeds, and when the wind was up, it whistled through the guide wires.

Some nights were black and forbidding, and others were as if gliding under a canopy of stars with only the slight movement of the funnels against the sky to indicate any perceptible motion. The sea might be still, have a low shadowy swell when seen in the moonlight or be frothy with white horses. On the last day out of New York, the air, warmed by the Gulf Stream, signalled summer ahead in New York.

On the final night, I wondered if I would have the chance to sail to Europe again, as I had done before I left England the last time aboard the *Queen Elizabeth*. Rounding the *Nantucket Lightship* symbolically marked the end as it was near familiar territory and the course was now a straight shot to *Ambrose*. But I was also happy, having received a letter from my parents before sailing that, after renting for 20 years, they had bought a house on the island of Nantucket, now only 45 miles away. It was the steamer to Nantucket in 1947 that gave me my first sea trip, albeit on an elderly day boat on a five-hour run. Now I was racing by the far side of the same island aboard the longest liner in the World.

Unable to sleep, I was up at 5:30 a.m. but we did not sail under the Verrazano Bridge until 8:30, passing six laid up troopships off Staten Island. An area of landfill replaced a line of finger piers just above where the United Fruit Company banana ships had docked. Other sheds were being pulled down for a huge project to build two enormous towers for a World Trade Center.

At Pier 40, where I had first worked for Holland America Line, the Norwegian America's *Sagafjord* and the Grace Line's *Santa Sofia* were tied up. The sidewheel steamboat *Alexander Hamilton* was nearly ready to sail from Pier 81 on an all-day trip up the Hudson, and the German *Hanseatic* and Italian *Raffaelo* were docked just above and just below the French Line pier.

Immigration took place on board, while chaos reigned on the pier. It was an hour and a half wait in the heat before the bags appeared under my letter. But I had the next stage of my life laid out, and now I had to sell the bill of goods to a school. I looked forward to that task, with trepidation. And as it turned out, I think I was hired on a bit of a whim. The headmaster, whose parents were missionaries, had been born not far from where I had briefly taught in Tanganyika, but I landed a job at one of the best private elementary schools in the country and stayed seven years.

ON BOARD THE *FRANCE*

The First Class smoking room.
Author's Collection.

A First Class outside cabin.
Author's Collection.

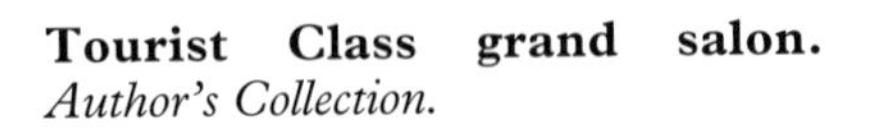

Tourist Class grand salon.
Author's Collection.

The Kennels were located on the Sun Deck. CGT issued pets' menus and thoughtfully provided a London lamp post, a French kilometer stone and a New York fire hydrant for the animals' convenience.
Charles N. Dragonette Collection.

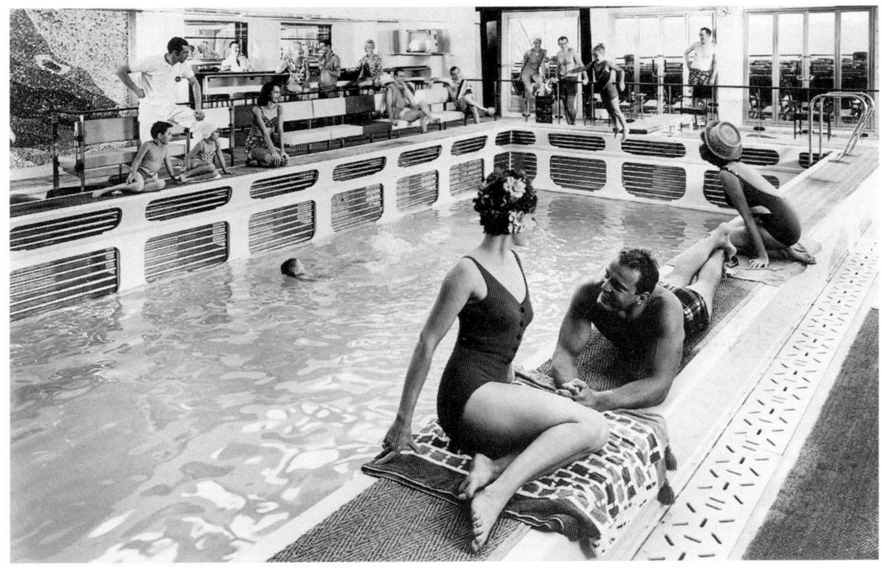

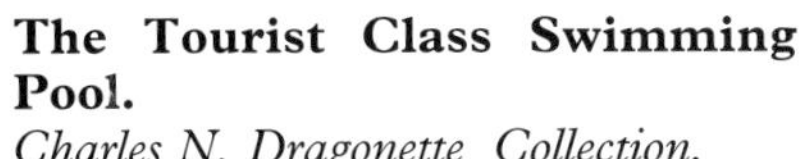

The Tourist Class Swimming Pool.
Charles N. Dragonette Collection.

First Class promenade deck.
Author's Collection.

Chapter Eight

Up the British Columbian Coast

MV Northland Prince

NORTHLAND NAVIGATION'S
MV NORTHLAND PRINCE
Vancouver-BC Ports-Vancouver March, 1969

The Canadian Province of British Columbia has a deeply indented coastline not unlike that of Norway. Many islands lie off to the west, including the Queen Charlotte Islands, an important chain located some distance into the Pacific Ocean, and Vancouver Island, stretching some 300 miles north-west from the tip of Washington State to parallel half of the BC coast.

Apart from a very large population centre at Vancouver in the south and the much smaller port city of Prince Rupert in the north, the mainland in the 1960s was largely underdeveloped. The rugged coastal terrain, numerous channels and deeply penetrating inlets and arms had prevented the construction of a continuous coastal highway.

To meet the province's transportation needs, large fleets of relatively small passenger and cargo ships once served the coastal communities and mining towns that sprang up along the inlets and on the islands. Today, vehicle ferries fill the gaps in the expanding provincial highway system and air travel provides a rapid alternative to many places, some of which would otherwise be completely isolated.

One does not have to turn the clock back very far, however, to recall the era when the combination passenger-cargo ship provided a useful service and an inexpensive way to see much of the World. In British Columbian waters, one such ship was the 3,800-ton, 110-passenger *Northland Prince*, which from 1963 to 1976 served as the flagship of the Northland Navigation Company.

Incorporated under this name in 1951 but tracing its origins back to 1941, Northland gradually expanded by acquiring units of the Canadian Pacific Railway, Union Steamship and Packers Steamship. In 1962, Phs.Van Ommeren NV, of Rotterdam, obtained a controlling interest in the seven ship-fleet, some cargo only and others taking up to 12 passengers. The *Northland Prince* became Northland's largest ship, making her maiden voyage from Vancouver on 11th June, 1963.

Locally built by the Burrard Dry Dock Co. at Vancouver, the 329-foot combination ship was powered by a 4,200 hp Stork-Werkspoor diesel engine capable of 16 knots and had three cargo holds with a 4,000 cubic ton capacity. The company, by then officially the Northland Navigation (1962) Co. Ltd., served no less than 130 ports along the BC Coast, on the north and the west coasts of Vancouver Island and in the Queen Charlotte Islands.

N

The *Northland Prince* provided a weekly year-round passenger, mail and cargo service from Vancouver to eight regular ports on the northbound voyage and made second calls at three of these on the southbound run. While the passenger berths in the summer months were sold out well in advance, off-season space was usually available at short notice and at reduced rates.

For the two-week spring break in March, 1969, the *Northland Prince* made an ideal choice, especially when combined with east-west transcontinental train journeys. The fare for a berth in a double cabin for six nights, including meals, was $120.

On Friday, 29th March, 1969 at 10:30pm, I started my journey at Grand Central Terminal in New York, occupying a Pullman berth aboard the *Montreal Limited* for the overnight journey to Montreal's Windsor Station. There I joined Canadian Pacific Railway's flagship train *The Canadian* for a three-day and three-night trip across Ontario, Manitoba, Saskatchewan and Alberta to Vancouver, British Columbia, arriving there on Tuesday afternoon, many hours late because of a derailment west of Fort William.

Approaching Vancouver along the Burrard Inlet, the CPR tracks passed close to the docked *Northland Prince*, her cargo booms swung out over the side. She looked small and dumpy compared to what I was used to seeing at the New York piers. Her red bottom appeared just above the waterline and her once green hull was now black. The accommodation was located aft in the white-painted superstructure. The squat red funnel had a black top band and a stylised black "N" placed on a white diamond. The *Northland Prince* was down at the stern, a characteristic pose she often took when docked and even underway.

It was well after dark when the taxi delivered me to the Northland Navigation pier for embarkation. The ship's cargo booms had finished loading and were neatly attached to the bipod masts. Two cars and several steel containers had been placed on the open forward deck. When I walked on board, a steward showed me to my cabin, an outside dark-panelled room with an upper and lower berth, a full-length sofa berth and adjoining private facilities with a shower. The cabin was certainly roomy but because of the relatively short nature of the voyage there was very little closet space and no chest of drawers. The 42 cabins fell into three categories, but all were outside with windows and full facilities. Apart from 12 deluxe rooms, with two lower beds and a sofa berth, the remaining cabins differed only in size and location.

The 65-seat dining room was located forward on B Deck facing the cargo gear and the holds. Had the ship been full there would have been a main and late sitting but on this early spring sailing the passenger count numbered 45, with half making the six-night voyage and others booked to way ports. The passengers were largely Canadians with a few Americans and British.

Above on C Deck there were two plain lounges, a small one facing aft through a semi-circular set of windows and the main lounge with a good unobstructed view ahead to the bow. The deck above had the bridge, sheltered seating beneath the lifeboats and an open deck aft. One set of stairs led up to open deck space aft of the funnel.

The *Northland Prince* sailed on time on Tuesday at 10 p.m. under a clear night sky. Leaving the harbour, the ship passed under the Lion's Gate suspension bridge linking North Vancouver with Vancouver. On the starboard side were the busy freight yards of the Pacific Great Eastern Railway while along the port side stretched the beautiful virgin woods of Stanley Park. Its shoreline footpath has always provided a wonderful vantage point for observing arriving and departing ships.

Once in the Strait of Georgia four consecutive nights aboard trains took effect and it was a pleasure to collapse into bed and be gently lulled to sleep by the quiet throb of the diesel engine.

Very early on Wednesday morning, the *Northland Prince* passed through the Seymour Narrows where the boiling tides can reach 14 knots, causing low-powered ships and tugs pulling barges to wait for more favourable conditions. While the passage was still cautiously considered, the treacherous twin peaks of Ripple Rock, blasted away by explosives in 1958, were no longer a hazard and ships now had a 50-foot clearance.

Tiny Kelsey Bay appeared to port. Located at the north end of Vancouver's main paved highway, the ferry port handled BC Ferries' *Queen of Prince Rupert*, making nightly sailings to and from Prince Rupert. The channel gradually widened between the heavily forested slopes of Vancouver Island and the mainland. At noon, we passed the northern tip of Vancouver Island and entered Queen Charlotte Sound with full exposure to the open Pacific Ocean. A slight swell gently lifted the ship but on occasion rough sea conditions can prevent the flat-bottomed Alaska Marine Highway ferries from attempting the two and one-half hour crossing until the sea moderates.

Shortly after entering the sound the *Northland Prince* veered northeast to enter the sheltered waters of Fitz-Hugh Sound, the Burke Channel, and the North Bentinck Arm. Some 80 miles inland, the ship approached the fishing village and lumber port of Bella Coola cast in the deep shadow of early evening. Several blasts from the ship's whistle, with following echoes, announced the weekly mailboat's arrival and soon a couple dozen cars were filing along the two-mile road linking Bella Coola with its wharf.

The town of 1,700 inhabitants is at the extreme end of a 300-mile gravel road leading off the main north-south provincial highway. During the two-hour call, nine passengers disembarked and a considerable amount of boxed food and crated machinery was off-loaded.

On the northbound run, the call at Ocean Falls, an isolated town of 3,000, was made well after midnight and I was not awake for any of the activity.

On Thursday morning, low-hanging gray clouds gripped the mountain sides bordering the Douglas Channel and nearly everyone remained inside reading, playing cards and chatting. Then about noon, in brightening skies, the *Northland Prince* docked at Kitimat, the aluminum centre of British Columbia and a relatively new town of 8,588 incorporated in 1951. The *Northland*

The *Northland Prince* is docked at the tiny British Columbian port of Butedale, located between Bella Coola and Kitimat. *Author's Collection.*

The *Northland Prince* at the mining town of Stewart, British Columbia, as far north as the ship could go on her domestic run. 29th March 1969. *Theodore W. Scull.*

Prince spent nearly 10 hours here discharging cargo before sailing at 10:30 p.m. for the overnight run to Prince Rupert. Once planned to be the principal Canadian west coast port, because of shorter steaming time to Japan and the Far East, Prince Rupert never took off and it ranks a distant second to Vancouver.

As we sailed at 2pm we passed the double-ended passenger and vehicle ferry to the city's Digby Island airport and the blue-striped, white hulled *Queen of Prince Rupert* docked just south of town

The *Northland Prince* sailed westward then northward, calling at Port Simpson, a remote Indian Reservation. During the brief stop, the local kids streamed aboard to buy sweets and sodas from the vending machines. Heading inland along Observatory Inlet, we called at tiny Kincolith and around midnight at Alice Arm, the site of an important molybdenum plant. None of these communities had road access to the outside world.

During the night the ship sailed up the parallel Portland Channel, bounded by the state of Alaska to port and the province of British Columbia to starboard. The town of Stewart, population 350, was as far north as the ship could go in British Columbia. Located at the southern end of a then uncompleted 400-mile road connecting with the Alaska Highway in the neighbouring Yukon Territory, the old copper mining town was in the throes of a long strike. Once the new contracts were in place, mining developers were planning on considerable expansion. During the call, I walked across the unprotected border into Hyder, Alaska, a virtual ghost town, and returned unchallenged.

Leaving Stewart at noon we took on some very drunk prospectors and collected some more at Alice Arm. The ship originally had a public bar but because of a rough element among the passengers the company removed it. However, alcoholic beverages could be consumed privately in the cabins, and they were.

The Saturday afternoon passage was breathtaking with steep snow-covered mountains plunging directly into the narrow channel. With feet up on the railing, I had a warm and sunny few hours on the open afterdeck. Though the ship was well inland, a school of porpoises followed her out to sea.

At this time, Northland Navigation was considering dropping nearly all the uneconomic ports from its schedules, except for Kitimat, Prince Rupert and Stewart, but when the company negotiated annual subsidies of $300,000, the calls at the remote outposts were maintained.

There was a short second stop at Prince Rupert on Saturday night and on Sunday morning we sailed up to Ocean Falls in daylight. Ocean Falls was well known for receiving 180 inches of rain a year and, true to its reputation, the heavens opened and a strong wind lashed at the ship as we sailed inland to Bella Coola. Several passengers, a white poodle and a crated St. Bernard, bound via the CNR for Saskatoon, came aboard.

The 22-hour run back to Vancouver included a wild passage through Queen Charlotte Sound and into the strait of the same name. The wind and limited visibility delayed the ship's arrival in Vancouver by several hours and it was after dark when the *Northland Prince* tied up at the Northland Dock, too late to begin discharging cargo until morning.

After spending a night in a Vancouver hotel, I booked a parlour observation car seat in Great Northern's *International* and left the CNR station for Seattle transferring to GN's *Empire Builder* occupying a duplex roomette in sleeping car *Bad Axe River*, for Chicago. A roomette in Penn Central's *Broadway Limited* took me overnight to Paoli, a suburban station outside Philadelphia, to celebrate a joint 1st April birthday with my Mother.

Over the next few years federal subsidies to Northland Navigation were gradually cancelled, first for service to the west coast of Vancouver Island and then entirely in 1976. In 1975 subsidies had reached $4.5 million and by then Northland was operating only three ships, the *Island Prince* (2), *Skeena Prince* and *Northland Prince*. The *Northland Prince* was finally laid up on 31st October 1976. The government tendered cargo, but not passenger, services to towing companies and Northland operated a tug and barge service until 1978 when the company finally expired.

In 1977, the *Northland Prince* was sold to the United International Bank of London, for less than $2 million for operation by Curnow Shipping of Cornwall. She left Vancouver for the last time on 4th November, 1977, carrying a load of lumber and destined to begin service as the *RMS St. Helena*. A ship that had spent nearly 15 years on the BC coast with only a few hours of each week exposed to the open sea would be making long voyages lasting nearly two months, sailing through the Bay of Biscay and the North and South Atlantic.

Happily, the little *Northland Prince*, which once had been a lifeline to isolated communities along the BC coast, would continue her vital role, trading to the even more remote islands of Ascension, St. Helena and Tristan da Cunha. When a brand- new, purpose-built *RMS St. Helena* entered service, the old *St. Helena* was briefly named *St. Helena Island*, then early in 1990 she was sold to Maltese-flag owners and renamed *Avalon*. She began operations for Sea Safaris on a passenger and cargo run from Durban to the Comoro Islands and the Seychelles. Cargo tonnage did not materialise in sufficient amounts, so the ship was laid up in Durban. In her last role, before the scrapyard, she was renamed *Indocéanique* for service from Mauritius to Réunion and other Indian Ocean islands.

In 1977 *Northland Prince* was sold to become the *St. Helena*, the link between the remote South Atlantic island of that name and the outside world. Note the tiny circular 'swimming pool'. *Laurence Dunn Collection.*

Chapter Nine

Inventing a New Cunard

RMS Queen Elizabeth 2

RMS QUEEN ELIZABETH 2
New York-Southampton June, 1969

After a first full year of teaching, I had three summer months to fill. The travel bug had bit hard after the around the World trip during the first half of 1968, so I arranged to sail to England, visit friends, then travel across Europe to Greece and come home from the Mediterranean. With the *Queen Elizabeth 2* finally in transatlantic service, I made a deposit for the minimum rate in a four-berth cabin at $295 half round trip, plus $2.10 port tax, by far the highest fare I had ever paid.

Then on 2nd May, the day the *QE2* sailed from Southampton on her maiden voyage, I made the final payment. While I missed her New York arrival, I went aboard the Staten Island Ferry on the afternoon of 9th May to see her sail out on the first eastbound crossing. She looked grand except for the tiny funnel carrying no Cunard colours.

My enthusiasm for ships had made its way into the classroom at St. Bernard's, and when the boys learned that I would be sailing on the *QE2*, everyone wanted to see me off. With the aid of a couple of parents I began planning a bon voyage party for 19th June. On the big day, the boys, some of their parents, my Mother, and several of my adult friends gathered in the Double Down Room, starboard side. Two or three boys would disappear at one time and come back with the latest find such as the room with pinball machines or the outdoor swimming pool but no water. But the most exciting place, and how they ever found them, were the dog kennels. Every kid had to go see the poor frightened pets cowering in the cages. The party was a huge success and cost nothing except for a nice tip to the steward.

The cabin listed on my ticket was 4009 but I got upgraded to 2019, my first ever twin-bedded accommodation shared with a total stranger. I was used to sleeping above or below my cabin mates but not side by side. My fate turned out to be an antique dealer twice my age who began to snore the moment his head hit the pillow. Happily, he was well aware of his problem and after two nights he managed to get a room on his own, and I now had mine, for the minimum fare thank you.

Unfortunately I fared even worse in the Britannia dining room. Having no table reservation, I went to the restaurant manager, and he placed me with a Union Pacific brakeman, his wife and teenage daughter who never spoke unless I started the conversation. These were days before one could escape to buffets but I managed to have breakfast in my cabin every morning.

Coincidentally, there were three St. Bernard's families, one colleague, a set of parents of another colleague, and my university history professor, so after hearing my tales of woe, I was invited to dinner on several nights. After marking up the passenger list, I counted 1884 names, making for a rather well-booked ship.

The *QE2* was so different from anything to date, and that is exactly what Cunard wanted, a complete break from the old Queens. While there were two classes, no one seemed to care where you went, except one night about 2 a.m. when I ordered some sandwiches in the Q4 Room. The response was very polite: I was welcome to stay but I could not be served any complimentary food.

I recognised various stewards from the old QE and knew which ones to avoid. While overall the service was good, there were some who were very poor, especially in the Britannia Restaurant, but part of that might have been attributed to a near capacity load on one of the first voyages. If I asked for anything special such as dressing for my salad, I got a long explanation from the steward about what he must do to get it for me.

Because of the open access, the variety of public rooms spread over three decks was staggering, and most of them had big windows looking out to the sea. The restaurants were situated well above the usual level, also with picture windows, an innovation for a passenger ship on the North Atlantic. Without two-deck high ceilings, apart from the Double Room, the spaciousness created by the large windows was very relieving.

I found that with the number of public rooms and entertainment venues available, passengers became widely dispersed. Most people did not seem to find a resting place as everyone was trying out different rooms. I was used to going to a certain bar at a certain time of the day and finding my crowd, but now unless you made an

The *Queen Elizabeth 2* in her original, 1969 form. *Laurence Dunn.*

The *Queen Elizabeth 2* arrives Pier 92, North River, New York on 18th June, 1969 and will turn around and sail the next day with the author on board. *Theodore W. Scull.*

Top left: **The author entertained his pupils at a bon voyage party before sailing.** *Author's Collection.*

Top right: **Cunard Pier 92 is packed with well-wishers on 19th June, 1969 seeing the *Queen Elizabeth 2* off on one of her inaugural season Atlantic crossings.** *Theodore W. Scull.*

Only a few weeks earlier, the *QE2*, as she rapidly became known, had sailed on her maiden voyage. Note the *QE2* logo in the top left hand corner *Author's Collection.*

appointment, you might not run into friends for a whole day or more. Some passengers seemed quite unsettled, even bored, not quite knowing what to do with themselves.

A five-day crossing passes very quickly for me, too much so, and I wanted more time to spend in my favorite rooms. Embarking with people I already knew helped, and for drinks before dinner, I liked the observation bar for its wonderful view over the bow from low-slung seats and the two little side rooms that could be reserved for private parties. Entertaining was cheap with several bar credits received as bon voyage gifts. The observation lounge had a good crowd before dinner but practically no business after the meal, and being off the main circulation trail, some passengers probably never found it.

Unfortunately, the room did not last very long and disappeared during one of the ship's many reconfigurations.

My other favorite was the Double Down Bar, aft of Double Room, and also under-utilised because of its out-of-the-way location. I liked ordering proper drinks here because the glass came with a double flag, Cunard White Star swizzle stick.

The Theatre Bar was the most lively place after hours, situated along a passage that on another ship would have been an enclosed Promenade Deck. The space seemed like an unfinished afterthought but it had a great atmosphere and a good singing quartet.

For reading, the Tourist Class Library was one of the best ever built into any ship. One could disappear into a

The *Queen Elizabeth 2* is steaming eastbound across the Atlantic on 22nd June, 1973. *Theodore W. Scull.*

deep-blue winged chair and when the eyelids got heavy, give in to sleep. The librarian, although I don't think he was trained as such, was a grump so I found it best to bring along my own books and avoid having anything to do with him. I tried to stay out of earshot as he could be so rude to passengers looking for help. This wonderful space did not last long either, so maybe he was put out to pasture.

Being a walker, I liked doing turns on the deck, and the *QE2* had a lengthy Boat Deck that substituted for a proper promenade, except that it did not make it all the way around on the same level. At the forward end, there were steps up and around the front of the superstructure then down again. With the ship doing 28 knots, plus head winds, one might have to battle hurricane forces, so most walkers, like myself, turned around after touching the stair railing. For safety reasons, the deck hands began putting up ropes to keep people from climbing the stairs and hung a sign that read "Danger High Winds."

On the last full day at sea, we experienced a complete power failure during lunch. The lights went out and slowly there was a perceptible change in the ship's movement until we were dead in the water and wallowing in a light swell. An announcement was made explaining that there had been a shut-down when a series of safety devices had activated in order to avoid the effects of an overload. Within an hour we were underway again, and that evening, Captain George Smith gave the passengers a complete explanation, which was much appreciated.

The *Queen Elizabeth 2* is docked at the Ocean Terminal in Southampton with Sitmar's *Fairsky* partially visible in the background. 31st August, 1973. *Theodore W. Scull.*

The next afternoon, we docked at Le Havre just ahead of the French liner *Antilles*, which soon after sailed past us for the West Indies. The boat train, now electrified, left for Paris St. Lazare with about 400 passengers, and we sailed across the Channel under our first clear skies and docked at Southampton at 1 a.m., right on schedule. Many sets of lights outlined other ships in port. Passengers were allowed to disembark but few did at this late hour.

At 6:45 a.m. I was on deck to view the scene. Royal Mail's *Andes* was in drydock with the former Cunarders *Carinthia* (now Sitmar *Fairland*) and *Sylvania* (*Fairwind*) tied up side by side, and Safmarine's *S.A. Vaal,* Union-Castle's *Pendennis Castle* and P&O's *Oriana* were bow to stern along the Western Docks. On the far side of the Ocean Terminal, Chandris' *Australis* was loading hold baggage for Australia, P&O's *Cathay* making ready for the Far East, the Swedish Lloyd's *Patricia* for Spain and *Vikings III* and *IV* for France. The Italian *Achille Lauro* was way off in the distance in drydock and the little *Duchesse de Normandie* on which I had sailed to the Channel Islands from France was laid up in bankruptcy.

Three boat trains were available, with the first leaving at 9:25 a.m., and we were to follow at 9:48, but due to delays in disembarkation, we did not depart until 11:20 behind the third, short boat train. The delay allowed me to wander the docks and photograph some of the ships close up.

Later, up in London, the *QE2* had made the front-page, "QUEEN BREAKS DOWN IN THE ATLANTIC." This was just one of the many headlines she would make over the years.

Over the years the *Queen Elizabeth 2* has become one of the most familiar sights in New York harbour. Here, on 18th January, 1981, she reverses in the icy North River at the start of her annual round-the-World cruise. *Theodore W. Scull.*

Seen from the Staten Island Ferry in Upper New York Bay, the *Queen Elizabeth 2* is outbound to Southampton on 11th September, 1981. *Theodore W. Scull.*

Chapter Ten

Italian Connections

MS San Marco & TSS Cristoforo Colombo

ADRIATICA'S *MS SAN MARCO*

Istanbul-Trieste August, 1969

The three-month period between mid-June and early September 1969 became my most intensive summer of ship travel ever. It began with that first voyage aboard the new *Queen Elizabeth 2*, followed by a night Channel crossing in Normandy Ferries' *Dragon*. Marseilles, during the height of the Mistral, provided some satisfying ship photography of the North African packets in their waning days, and a train journey down the Italian peninsula ended at Brindisi where I chose to sail Efthymiades from a line of eager shipping agents who met the trains. The elderly 1,630-ton *Ledra I*, jammed with backpackers, had an engine failure the next morning off the coast of Albania, and we drifted in heavy seas for several hours before getting under way again for Patras. At the time, the American passport did not permit travel to Albania, so I wondered what would happen if we landed on the beach.

The month and a day touring Athens, Piraeus, the Peloponnese and the Greek Islands included overnight voyages on two quickly-converted former Messageries Maritimes liners, *Jean Laborde* and *Ferdinand de Lesseps*, which had been built in the early 1950s to trade deep into the Indian Ocean.

Istanbul was as far east as I would go, and one final link remained to be organised in order to reach Trieste by the 26th August to join the *Cristoforo Colombo* for the westbound crossing to New York. Adriatica Line had the perfect connection but the *San Marco* was fully booked in both classes, and I was wait-listed.

In the meantime there were alternatives to consider. The Direct Orient Express from Sirkeci Station, near to where I was staying, had a twice-a-week sleeping car and it was also full. Second class meant two nights sitting up in a packed compartment on what had become a local train for migrants. Turkish Maritime Lines' car ferry *Truva* left from Izmir, a whole day's journey away, for Venice, while TML's express passenger service and the Soviet Black Sea Line went to Naples on the wrong side of Italy.

Between shipping office calls, an amazing array of overseas tonnage came and went from the impressive maritime station, and Turkish Maritime Lines' own resident fleet, docked bow to stern, presented a handsome sight against the skyline. On the morning I arrived on the Turkish liner *Izmir* from Rhodes, my notes recorded Costa's *Andrea C.* and the Bulgarian *Nessebar* lying alongside, and the next day produced Epirotiki's *Jason*, the Romanian *Transylvania* and the Turkish *Ege*, *Eturk*, and *Tirhan*, with the giant P&O *Canberra* at anchor. Following a day away up the Bosphorus visiting friends, the lineup included the Bulgarian *Georgi Hirov*, the Greek *Orion*, the Italian *San Marco*, the ship I had hoped to board, and the TML's *Akdeniz*.

Two days before the *San Marco* was due to sail, I called in at the Adriatica office, and a late cancellation produced a first-class outside single with washbasin. The accommodation was a considerable step up from a six-berth cabin in third class aboard the *Izmir*. The fare came to $156.50 with taxes and a 15 per cent educator's reduction, and I walked out with a passage ticket that read Prof. Theodore Wiedersheim SCULL.

On sailing day, the maritime station was chaotic with embarking and disembarking passengers, their well-wishers, heaps of baggage, porters, and a phalanx of uniformed officials. Through the windows, I spied the copper green, winged Venetian lion set stylishly against the *San Marco*'s orange-yellow funnel. Completed in 1956, the 4,755-ton ship and her sister, the *San Giorgio*, had a service speed of 17 knots. The two alternated on the Turkey-Greece-Italy route with the *San Marco* going up the Adriatic side to Bari, Venice and Trieste, and the *San Giorgio* sailing around the heel and toe to Naples, Marseilles and Genoa. This service and two others serving

Cyprus, Israel, Lebanon and Egypt were timed to connect with the Italian ships to North, Central and South America.

Originally designed with three classes, the *San Giorgio* and *San Marco* had recently combined second and tourist classes into a larger tourist with just over 100 berths while first carried just under 100. The ships had two cargo holds forward and two aft, and while underway one was rigged as the outdoor swimming pool.

A delightful Cabin 138 on D Deck had a single bed placed under a porthole, a washbasin, chest of drawers and closet with a bath and two showers located just across the corridor. The first-class public rooms were arranged along B Deck with a spacious observation lounge forward joined to a small semi-circular bar alcove, both rooms with slightly elevated ceilings. Through the windows, I watched cars being crane-loaded and stowed on deck either side of the two cargo hatches. A starboard side gallery, serving as a card and writing room, led aft to a dining room with great views to the side and over the stern through three-foot diameter portholes.

Tourist-class public rooms were arranged on the deck below from midships aft with one dining room here and another with high density seating another level down, reflecting the original three-class design. Deck space was limited to side promenades and a small lido around the pool.

We sailed at 1 p.m., easing away from the stern of the Bulgarian *Nessebar* and once in the stream, the day's ship roster included Paquet's *Ancerville,* Black Sea's *Uzbekistan* and the Turkish *Akdeniz*, *Izmir*, *Marmara*, *Girsun*, *Ordu* and *Ayvalik*. Besides the big ships, there were dozens of rakish local steamers and double-ended car ferries, many throwing off plumes of coal smoke as they crossed the Bosphorus against a backdrop of St. Sophia, the Blue Mosque, Topkapi Palaces and the Galata Tower.

The *San Marco* sailed through the wide Sea of Marmara and into the narrowing Dardanelles flanked by forts and the Anzac Memorial to World War I Australian and New Zealander losses at Gallipoli.

The first-class passengers were mostly from Western Europe, while in tourist one found the people who

Adriatica's express passenger-cargo liner *San Marco* at Venice. *Adriatica Line.*

An 18th August, 1969 scene down by the docks in Istanbul showing the Romanian liner *Transylvania* and Turkish Maritime's *Tirhan*. *Theodore W. Scull.*

provided labour for the countries where the first-class resided, plus students and travellers on the cheap.

My dining companion at a table for two was a much older, affable Turkish Cypriot who taught school in England and travelled every summer between London and Limassol via train and the ships of Adriatica and Turkish Maritime lines. He had definite opinions on politics, and we kept the peace after I took up the role of an interested listener rather than attempting to hold up my end.

The menus were printed in French and Italian but certain entrées such as Roast Beef à la Windsor and spaghetti translated rather easily on both panels. The food was excellent, and the captain's dinner featured caviar, smoked salmon, lobster (probably tinned and not a great success), pheasant, a special cake, and at midnight following the dance and horse racing, Champagne and crêpes suzettes. The ambiance was Italian-flavoured French Line in miniature.

Retiring well after midnight, I switched off the air-conditioning and swung open the porthole. I lay back and realised that this was the first time I had ever slept in a dedicated single cabin. There was no snoring, noisy early risers and late nighters or sounds of the city.

We docked at Izmir for the day from where I went off to the glorious ruins at Ephesus, which must be the most extensive site in the ancient world, and the following morning, we sailed into Piraeus, a tight harbour choked with domestic and overseas Greek shipping. There was, however, but one foreign ship, the pretty little Egyptian passenger vessel *Syria*.

The highlight of the voyage came as we approached the Corinth Canal, a short cut through the Peloponnese used by relatively small ships making for the Adriatic. We waited for the Israeli car ferry *Dan*, en route from Venice to Haifa, to clear, then allowed the Greek-flag *Kolokotronis* to overtake us, and what a sight she was. The 1,800-ton ship, one of the few that sailed directly between Brindisi and Piraeus rather than to Patras, was well loaded with student-age passengers, many seated in lifeboats. She

Looking forward over cars stowed on the deck of the *San Marco* to the Bulgarian liner *Nessebar* (formerly C.G.T.'s *Ville de Bordeaux* and Swedish Lloyd's *Saga*) and the Soviet Black Sea *Uzbekistan* at Istanbul on 21st August, 1969. *Theodore W. Scull.*

First class on the *San Marco* and her sister *San Giorgio* was particularly pleasant. Here is the verandah lounge. *Adriatica Line.*

resembled a refugee ship except that everyone aboard wore broad smiles and cheerfully shouted across the open water.

Being much smaller, the *Kolokotronis* went ahead unassisted, then with tugs fore and aft, the *San Marco* began the one-hour airless transit between heat-radiating rock walls. The ship took on two pilots, one barking orders to the helmsman and the other moving frequently from bridge wing to bridge wing to the eye the clearance of a scant few feet. People waved from a road bridge and a blue diesel train passed overhead en route to the Peloponnese.

Breaking out into the Gulf of Corinth, we sailed past Delphi and overnight up the hazy Adriatic to the industrial port of Bari. The one-hour call stretched to three with much cargo to unload and cars to take on for people who wished to avoid the long drive up the coast. Arriving Venice by sea is a marvellous experience, passing the Lido, San Marco Square and the entrance to the Grand Canal. The pier was within walking distance of the centre, though the way proved to be a confusingly complex maze of alleys, bridges and canals. Most passengers disembarked leaving only 20 in first class for the final leg to Trieste.

Had the ship arrived Trieste at 10 p.m. as scheduled, it would have meant disembarking and searching for a hotel before returning to the pier the next morning to board the *Cristoforo Colombo*. Happily, we left Venice six hours late, which meant a Trieste arrival the following morning.

A ship with two names, the Greek *Georges Potamianos* was also called the *Kolokotronis*. Here, crowded with students, she is overtaking the *San Marco* to head into the Corinth Canal on 23rd August, 1969.
Theodore W. Scull.

ITALIA'S *TSS CRISTOFORO COLOMBO*
Trieste-New York August-September, 1969

Through the drizzly half darkness I could see the *Colombo* lit up against a sleeping city that spread over low hills in an arc around the bay. Several old hotels and the huge rectangular Lloyd Triestino headquarters dominated the otherwise dreary skyline. After an unexpected bonus of a call to breakfast, I disembarked and walked the short distance to my liner bound for New York.

The *Cristoforo Colombo* and its 13-day route was a bargain, because whether one embarked in Trieste, Venice, Messina, Palermo, Naples or Malaga (six days after leaving Trieste) the fare remained the same. The only exception was Piraeus, the call between Venice and Messina, because the Transatlantic Steamship Conference placed it in a more easterly fare zone.

My parents had loved their 1955 crossing on the *Andrea Doria* which they had found as much fun as the French Line, so I took their cue and booked her near-sister.

Completed at Genoa in 1954, the *Colombo* was 29,429 tons, and carried approximately 300 in first, 240 in cabin and 700 in tourist classes, figures that varied with interchangeable accommodations. Now that the US immigration restrictions had been substantially reduced, the Italian Line ships were again carrying thousands of westbound migrants to Halifax and New York. It seemed wise to pay extra for cabin class, berth 512A in an outside four berth on B Deck with en suite shower. However, being so close to the waterline, the deadlights were in place, and the cabin was in effect an inside.

While the *Colombo* presented a handsome profile, my first reaction upon embarking was of a rather dowdy interior coupled with a feeling of being sandwiched between the grand class above and the tight quarters below. Cabin class had two undistinguished lounges on Promenade Deck and a much finer Boat Deck verandah bar facing an after pool. Promenade space was limited to short sections on these two decks. With the three classes

The Italian Line's *Cristoforo Colombo* is maneuvering past San Marco Square in Venice. *Author's Collection.*

The *Cristoforo Colombo* at Venice on the 26th August, 1969. *Theodore W. Scull.*

more or less separated vertically, one was always running into barriers, but after a few days, I found my way both above and below my class and no one seemed to take much notice.

Sailing from Trieste at 10 a.m., we arrived Venice at 2:45 p.m. for a three-hour call. With very little clearance, the departure was especially tricky and two tugs were needed at both the bow and stern to turn the ship 180 degrees. The ship, looming over the low-rise city, must have presented quite a sight from San Marco Square, the spot from where I had seen the *Saturnia* pass in 1960.

After a hazy day at sea, the night air cleared and I stayed up by the mast until 3:00 a.m. watching the outline of the coast under the half light of a near full moon.

The *Cristoforo Colombo* was a mighty large ship to bring into Piraeus especially using what appeared to be under-powered tugs, and we stayed the morning, sailing again at 1 p.m. By dawn the following day the coast of Sicily appeared and Mt Aetna smoked in the distance. Threading amidst Italian State Railway ferries shuttling between Sicily and Italy's toe, the *Colombo* docked alongside the centre of Messina. Many men and women seeing off relatives to Canada and America were dressed in black, and lots of tears flowed at sailing time.

We steamed through the rip tides and whirlpools of Charybdis then passed under the rocky promontory of Scylla as the ancient Greeks had done with much less horsepower. Again in open water, we turned west toward Palermo between Sicily's north coast and two volcanic Lipari Islands rising out of the sea. While more migrants

Tearful farewells at Messina as the *Cristoforo Colombo* embarks emigrants for Halifax and New York, 29th August, 1969. *Theodore W. Scull.*

The first class open promenade deck on the *Cristoforo Colombo* was spacious enough to be a car park and a deck where passengers could walk their dogs. *Theodore W. Scull.*

boarded here, the ship laid on a short tour to a Byzantine-style church high above the city featuring beautiful mosaics and a painted wooden ceiling. Sailing at midnight, I went straight to bed to be prepared for the long day at Naples.

The ship passed through the breakwater at 7:30 a.m. and docked at the huge 1930s Maritime Station opposite the beautiful *Leonardo da Vinci,* a replacement for the *Andrea Doria,* and the equally fine-looking *Galileo Galilei,* one of a fast pair built for Lloyd Triestino's Australian service, both prides of the Italian merchant marine.

I took a local train out to Herculaneum, a 2,000-year-old resort city that had two days' warning before being covered in lava following the eruption of Mt. Vesuvius in 79 A.D. Here much was preserved, while Pompeii was rained on by burning cinders and ash.

The *Michelangelo* arrived at midday, reversing into the berth, her decks packed with people. Shortly, the handsome *Akdeniz* of Turkish Maritime Lines and the graceful gray-hulled *Isthmia,* originally Swedish Lloyd's *Suecia* of 1929, came into port. Also docked was Tirrenia's oldest ship, the 1930-built *Città di Tunisi,* now operating on the Naples-Sicily-Malta-Tripoli (Libya) run. It was quite a catch and the photographic conditions were superb. The weather turned extraordinarily humid during the next day at sea and by evening a terrific series of thunderstorms swept across the ship. Standing out on the Boat Deck, the lightning turned night into day. It was frightening and yet exciting, and a passing officer said not to worry as the ship was well earthed.

The next morning we wallowed off Malaga in the rain and heavy swells, and after two hours standing off, the captain abandoned the call and sailed to Algeciras to embark passengers. The weather cleared as the ship sailed past Gibraltar to drop anchor in the bay. About 4 p.m., a passenger tender came out to embark 40 and disembark 90. A barge pulled alongside and four cars were crane-loaded aboard and seven taken off.

Three vehicles ended up being parked on the Boat Deck, and at a designated hour each morning several passengers had permission to walk their poodles along this same deck. Like clockwork, the car owners would also appear and would lean, with folded arms, against their prize possessions to ward off any chance of lifting legs.

Upon entering the Atlantic, I developed one heck of a sore throat and a temperature. The surgery was helpful with antibiotics but I made the mistake of going out by the pool on transatlantic day two. In the middle of the night, I awoke with a burning fever and set off to find the doctor, ending up quite lost in the steel plated crew quarters. A night steward saw my sweaty state, summoned a nurse who took me directly to the surgery. After taking my temperature, she phoned the doctor, handed me a new set of pills and escorted me back to the cabin with orders to stay there. I was sufficiently recovered two days later to go outside during the docking at Halifax but not off the ship.

Two familiar faces appeared on a companionway, and stunned, I was not sure whether they were real or I was still hallucinating. In fact, they both were ship-related friends from New York, one of whom, 30 years later, has contributed to this book. The two-night trip between Halifax and New York had once been a popular short voyage, and empty berths were always available, especially in tourist with migrants disembarking. Then the one-way fare was $35 in tourist, $55 in cabin and $70 in first.

The New York arrival was very gloomy with low clouds and heavy smog, but I was glad to be back home 84 days after sailing over on the *Queen Elizabeth 2.* Less than 48 hours later, I was back at St. Bernard's meeting my new class, all of whom seemed to know about the sailing party in June. Where was sir going next summer?

Italian passenger ships at Naples on the 30th August, 1969.

(Opposite) the Italian Line's *Leonardo da Vinci*, and (below) Lloyd Triestino's *Galileo Galilei*.
Theodore W. Scull.

(Above) the Italian Line's *Michelangelo* and (opposite) Tirrenia's elderly *Città di Tunisi*. *Theodore W. Scull.*

Epilogue

In late 1998, only four of the dozen steamship lines featured here remain in business. Holland America is going gangbusteres as a major cruise ship operator under the Carnival Corporation banner; while Cunard languished for many years under two owners before Carnival took a majority interest in 1998 and announced plans to expand the company. In 1970, North German Lloyd merged with Hamburg America to form Hapag-Lloyd and now operates several cruise ships and an important fleet of container vessels. Adriatica, whose handsome fleet spanned the Mediterranean, is but a shadow of itself, engaged in mostly local and overnight ferry runs. The once mighty French Line (Compagnie Générale Transatlantique), merged into the Compagnie Générale Maritime in 1977, and the Italian Line, now simply Italia, operates only cargo container services. Hamburg Atlantic, Swedish American, Swedish Lloyd, Royal Mail, Navigation Mixte and Northland Navigation are but distant memories.

Five of the featured ships remain in service although only one, the *Queen Elizabeth 2*, has retained her name and dual purpose, presently the sole liner in transatlantic service and also a cruise ship. The *France*, withdrawn in 1974 and laid up at Le Havre, re-entered cruise service in 1980 as the rebuilt *Norway* for Norwegian Caribbean Lines, now Norwegian Cruise Line. She remains the longest liner at 1,035 feet, but has been outclassed as the World's largest cruise ship by new tonnage.

The *Rotterdam* abandoned the North Atlantic for full-time cruising in 1969 and carried on with great success until October, 1997 when Holland America sold her to Premier Cruises who operate her as the largely unchanged *Rembrandt*. As the *Rotterdam*, she made more World cruises and visited more ports than any passenger ship in history.

Cunard sold the *Sylvania* in 1968, and the Sitmar Line operated her as the *Fairwind*, much rebuilt for cruise service. In 1988 when P&O/Princess absorbed Sitmar, she became the *Dawn Princess* but now operates primarily for the German market as the *Albatros* under the management of V-Ships.

Swedish Lloyd's *Patricia* has had many changes of ownership and name - *Stena Saga*, *Lion Queen*, *Crown Princess Victoria*, *Pacific Star*, *Sun Fiesta* - and has operated as a short sea day and overnight ferry liner and gambling ship in Scandinavia, North America and now the Far East.

Adriatica's pretty little cargo-passenger liner *San Marco* became the victim of changing trade requirements. She was rebuilt as the *City of Myconos*, cruising in the Mediterranean until laid up, sinking at her moorings in late 1995.

The scrapyard has been the final destination for most of the others, but in a few cases a fire prematurely ended a career and one ship sank under tow en route to the breakers.

Cunard's *Queen Elizabeth* was withdrawn in 1968 and for about a year was tied up at Port Everglades as a tourist attraction. When the owners went bankrupt, Chinese shipping tycoon C. Y. Tung bought her with the intention of operating her as a floating university ship *Seawise University*. However, she caught fire, probably sabotage, and burned out in Hong Kong in 1972. While some of the wreckage was removed, the rest remained and is now buried under new dock construction.

The French Line's *Liberté*, built way back in 1930 as North German Lloyd's *Europa*, was withdrawn at the end of 1961 just before the advent of the *France*, and scrapped in 1962. In 1962, the *Flandre* left North Atlantic service for the West Indies route until 1968 when she was sold to Costa and rebuilt to become their very successful *Carla C.*, later *Carla Costa*. With the arrival of Costa newbuilds, Epirotiki took her on as their *Pallas Athena*. She caught fire at Piraeus in March, 1994, suffered extensive damage and was scrapped later that year. The *Flandre*'s memory lives on as a one-metre-long ship model I purchased at Christie's, New York in early 1998.

The French Line's Mediterranean service was merged with Navigation Mixte in 1969 and gradually the fast packet ships were withdrawn in favour of car ferries. The handsome *Ville de Marseille* (1952) lasted only 21 years until scrapped in 1973, while the *Sampiero Corso* of 1936 traded for 30 years until scrapped in 1966. Navigation Mixte's *Président de Cazalet* of 1947 became Efthymiades' *Arcadi* and, after the collapse of that company, endured a long lay-up before being scrapped.

North German Lloyd's *Bremen* sailed just 12 years on the North Atlantic before being sold to Chandris in 1971 to become *Regina Magna*. She sank while under tow to the scrapyard as the *Filipinas Saudi I* in 1980.

The *Hanseatic*, dating from 1930, caught fire in New York in 1966, an event I viewed with considerable sadness. She was deemed too badly damaged to be repaired and was scrapped the same year.

Swedish American's *Kungsholm* of 1953 was sold to North German Lloyd in 1964, in anticipation of a new *Kungsholm*, and traded as the *Europa*, then after 1981 as the *Columbus C.* for Costa. In 1984 she struck the breakwater at Cadiz and sank at her berth. She was raised and sold to Spanish breakers in 1985, and I saw her under tow in the western Mediterranean while travelling aboard the *Canberra* en route from Sydney to Southampton.

The Italian Line's *Cristoforo Colombo* operated on the North Atlantic from 1953 to 1977 when she was sold to become an accomodation ship in Venezuela. In 1981, she was towed to the Far East. It was briefly hoped she might find further employment but she was scrapped in 1983.

Royal Mail's *Amazon* lasted only eight years on the South American run, then transferred within the Furness Withy Group to become Shaw Savill's *Akaroa* for a further three years on the long liner service between Britain and Australia and New Zealand. She was rebuilt into a car transport before being scrapped in 1981.

The later career of the passenger-cargo ship *Northland Prince* was well covered in the text, but it is worth repeating that she had one of the most remarkable operational changes of any ship, from trading along the protected British Columbia coast to the long open sea route from Britain deep into the South Atlantic to serve three of the World's most remote islands as Curnow Shipping's RMS *St. Helena*.

The author back home in New York. *Marguerite O'Neill*

Index